The
Christian Latin Literature
of the First Six Centuries

# THE CATHOLIC LIBRARY OF RELIGIOUS KNOWLEDGE

*Translated from the French*

### PRELIMINARY LIST

Baptism and Confirmation. Rev. A. D'Alès, S.J.
The Breviary. Its History and Contents. Dom Baudot, O.S.B.
The Church in Modern Times, 1447-1789. Canon Léman.
The Cradle of the Bible. Mgr. Legendre.
The Moral Law of the Family. P. Méline.
The Last Things. Abbé A. Michel.
St. Paul. Abbé Tricot.
The Papacy. Abbé F. Mourret.
Holiness in the Church. R. Plus, S.J.
The Foundations of Thomistic Philosophy.
R. P. Sertillanges, O.P.
Greek Literature in the Early Church. Abbé G. Bardy.
The Christian Latin Literature of the First Six Centuries.
Abbé G. Bardy.
The Congregations of Priests, XVI—XVIII Century.
Canon Pisani.
Creation and Evolution. Canon Sendrens.
The Church in the Early Centuries. Abbé Amann.
The Theology of the New Testament. R. P. Lemonnyer, O.P.
Pastors and People. Canon Magnin.
Religious Music. Abbé Aigrain.

**Catholic Library of Religious Knowledge**

XII

# The Christian Latin Literature of the First Six Centuries

BY
ABBÉ BARDY

TRANSLATED BY
MOTHER MARY REGINALD, O.P.

**Nihil Obstat**
JOANNES GRAY
*Censor Deputatus.*

**Imprimatur**
✢ JOSEPH
*Archiep. S. Andr. et Edim.*

EDIMBURGI,
*die 14 Januarii, 1930*

# CONTENTS

|  | PAGE |
|---|---|
| INTRODUCTION . . . . . . | 1 |

## FIRST PERIOD

### THE BEGINNINGS (SECOND AND THIRD CENTURIES)

SUMMARY . . . . . . . 17

### CHAPTER I
#### THE BEGINNINGS

I. Translations. II. First Attempts . . . 19

### CHAPTER II
#### TERTULLIAN AND MINUCIUS FELIX

I. Tertullian's Life. II. His Works. III. Minucius Felix . . . . . . . 28

### CHAPTER III
#### SAINT CYPRIAN AND HIS CONTEMPORARIES

I. The Writings of Saint Cyprian. II. Novatian. III. Saint Cyprian's Contemporaries. IV. Commodianus . . . . . 40

v

# CONTENTS

## CHAPTER IV
### THE DAWN OF THE FOURTH CENTURY

I. Arnobius. II. Lactantius. III. Reticius and Victorinus . . . . . . . 53

## SECOND PERIOD
### THE APOGEE (313-430)

SUMMARY . . . . . . . 69

## CHAPTER V
### SCHISMS AND HERESIES

I. Donatism. II. Arianism. III. Victorinus. IV. Lucifer. V. Saint Hilary . . . . 71

## CHAPTER VI
### SAINT AMBROSE AND HIS FRIENDS

I. Saint Ambrose. II. His Contemporaries . . 88

## CHAPTER VII
### SAINT JEROME AND HIS TIME

I. Life of Saint Jerome. II. The Works of Saint Jerome. III. Rufinus. IV. Other Writers . 99

# CONTENTS

### CHAPTER VIII
#### CHRISTIAN POETRY IN THE FOURTH CENTURY
I. Various Poets. II. Saint Paulinus of Nola. III. Prudentius . . . . . . . 119

### CHAPTER IX
#### SAINT AUGUSTINE
I. Life of Saint Augustine. II. His Works . . 130

### CHAPTER X
#### FRIENDS AND ENEMIES OF SAINT AUGUSTINE
I. Saint Augustine's Adversaries. II. His Friends . 146

## THIRD PERIOD
### THE BARBARIAN TIMES (430-636)

SUMMARY . . . . . . . 157

### CHAPTER XI
#### AUGUSTINISM
I. Saint Prosper. II. Saint Cassian. III. The Lérinians. IV. Other Writers. V. Saint Leo the Great . . . . . . 159

### CHAPTER XII
#### THE LAST POETS OF ANTIQUITY
I. Gallic Poets. II. Sidonius Apollinaris. III. Sedulius and Dracontius. IV. Saint Avitus and Ennodius. V. Fortunatus . . . 170

# CONTENTS

## CHAPTER XIII

### BARBARIAN AND BYZANTINE AFRICA

                                                                                 PAGE

I. The Barbarian Period. II. Byzantine Controversies . . . . . . 182

## CHAPTER XIV

### ITALY

I. Secondary Writers. II. Boethius. III. Cassiodorus. IV. Saint Gregory the Great . . 189

## CHAPTER XV

### GAUL AND SPAIN

I. Theologians and Controversialists. II. Saint Gregory of Tours. III. The Spaniards. IV. Saint Isidore of Seville . . . . 202

CONCLUSION . . . . . . 215

BIBLIOGRAPHY . . . . . . 221

# The Christian Latin Literature
## of the First Six Centuries

### INTRODUCTION

It was not until nearly the end of the second century that the Latin-speaking Christians began to produce works fit for inclusion in a history of literature. Up to that time they had only possessed rather literal translations of the Bible, or at least of its principal portions, and some other Greek writings, which, on their first appearance, had been received with respect and attained sufficient popularity to justify their almost immediate translation into the vernacular. But after the year 190 they were no longer content with these translations and there rose up amongst them original writers who at once produced masterpieces which secured to Christian thought in the West the possession of a complete and perfect language; so much so that those who, especially in Rome, endeavoured to perpetuate the ancient custom and continued to write in Greek, appeared before long as foreigners and were misunderstood by their own compatriots.

These facts, which had important consequences,

## THE CHRISTIAN LATIN LITERATURE OF

command the attention of all who would understand the future of Christian Latin literature, for they indicate from the outset its definite orientation. Little as we know of the circumstances of the evangelization of the West, we may be certain that those who bore the Good Tidings thither were Orientals; Jews of Palestine, Syria and Asia Minor, or converted pagans from the same regions, all speaking Greek and addressing themselves to their brethren of race and tongue before preaching to the Latins. The list of persons saluted by S. Paul towards the end of his Epistle to the Romans enlightens us to some extent as to who were the members of the Roman community about the year 60: by the side of some Latin names we there find a majority of Greek persons whose names are attested by the inscriptions in Asia Minor. Again, the list of the martyrs of Lyons in 177 shows us that this newly-born Christian community comprised more Asiatics than Latins or Celts. It was therefore natural that the first writings addressed to Churches whose members regarded Greek as their mother-tongue should have been composed in that language. The Epistle of S. Paul to the Romans, the *Pastor* of Hermas, the *Adversus Hæreses* of S. Irenæus—to say nothing of S. Clement's *Letter*, which, addressed to the Corinthians, would naturally be written in Greek—mark some of the chief stages in the Christian thought of the West. To this may be added the fact that in the first and second centuries of our era the Greek language was so widely spread in the Mediterranean countries that it was generally used even by the lower classes of Rome, Carthage and Marseilles, whilst the historians and philosophers, even though they were emperors, like

## THE FIRST SIX CENTURIES

Marcus Aurelius, willingly employed it in order to give a wider circulation to their writings. When an Apologist, settled in Rome, like S. Justin, wished to present the Emperor and the Sacred Senate with an address in defence of the Faith he wrote in Greek, not only because he himself was a Palestinian, but still more because he knew that thus he would please the powerful ones of the day.

Nevertheless we must not think that Christianity remained in the West an exotic religion and that its chief members were recruited only from the Oriental colonies. On the contrary we know that it spread very early amongst those of Latin race and that before the middle of the second century these held a conspicuous position in the Roman community. Perhaps the heretics were the first to realize the influence they might gain if they addressed themselves to the natives in their own tongue; at least it is probable that the most ancient Latin translations of the New Testament emanated from Marcion or his disciples. But the Church did not long allow heresy to profit by this advantage; very soon the faithful were given Latin versions of the Bible, the *Doctrine* of *the Apostles*, the *Letter* of *S. Clement to the Corinthians* and the *Pastor* of Hermas.

The function of these translations was decisive in the formation of the Christian Latin language. Their authors were not literary men, anxious to clothe in fine words the oracles of the prophets, the Epistles of S. Paul, or the Gospels of the Apostles; their sole anxiety was to provide their brethren of race and tongue with the means of reading the Sacred Books that contained the divine revelation. Without much instruction themselves, they translated as literally as possible and did not fear to use familiar expressions, popular terms, constructions that were incorrect in the judgment of grammarians; and, when Latin words failed them, they would make use of simple transcriptions of Greek formulas. The Septuagint Bible and the New Testament had already been written in the language of the common people, bristling with vulgarisms and studded with Jewish idioms, and the first Latin versions of the Bible preserved and even added to this crudity. There was thus introduced into the language of literature—that, at least, to which the Christians were to become accustomed—new terms with hitherto unacceptable meanings, and in some cases broader rules of syntax than those of the classical authors. Whilst possessing no official character, these versions were imposed upon the different Christian assemblies; they furnished writers with innumerable quotations, and they largely inspired the style and vocabulary of the literature of the future. In vain did men of letters protest over and over again during the succeeding centuries against the barbarisms of these translations. Christian writers ceased not to defend them, and S. Jerome himself, when he undertook to present the world with a new version of the Bible, founded on the Hebrew text, cared only to keep close to the truth of the original and did not trouble himself to produce a work of art.

Though the most ancient translations of the Sacred Books first saw the light in Rome, that city was nevertheless not destined to give birth to the earliest original Latin writers. This glory was reserved for Carthage, and the position held by Africa from the beginning, in the history of Latin

## THE FIRST SIX CENTURIES

literature, claims our attention without further delay.

The most ancient author who wrote in Latin appears to have been Pope Victor, a native of Africa according to the *Liber Pontificalis*; but none of his *opuscula* have been preserved. Then, too, Tertullian was his contemporary, and his name is sufficient to characterize an epoch.

This latter was a great writer. He had gone deeply into classical studies before his conversion, and however forcibly he might reproach the pagan poets and philosophers, he retained in the depths of his heart the enchantment of the beauty and harmony that Cicero and Virgil had revealed to him. He knows how a period should be constructed; he understands, like a rhetorician, the force of a phrase, and the orator's art has no secrets for him. Above all, he possessed that innate eloquence which nothing can replace. He had been gifted by Providence with a lively and vivid imagination, ardent and enthusiastic passions, a penetrating intelligence, and he used all these gifts magnificently. It is easy to recognize in him the qualities and defects of the typical African: a sometimes excessive ardour; an often exaggerated transport; the love of outlandish expressions and violently striking formulas. But he devoted all the energies of his fiery and exuberant nature without reserve to the service of Christianity, first as a Catholic, and towards the end of his life amidst the errors of Montanism. Thus, whilst the Greek Christians were awaiting their first writer of talent, those of the Latin tongue could pride themselves on the possession of Tertullian as an incomparable master.

His influence was enormous; he taught his coreligionists the value of literary work and the force which can be given to an idea by clothing it in suitable words, and the West did not forget the lesson. S. Cyprian, also a native of Carthage, was a disciple of the great orator, for whose works he was constantly asking. In the midst of the struggles that troubled his episcopate he found time to write letters and treatises from which none of the ornaments of style are banished, and where the rhythmic phrases betray a perpetual seeking after harmony. What a contrast there is between the letters of this great bishop and those which, after the death of Pope Fabian, were written to him by the priests of Rome, who had not yet learnt to use the pen of a Novatian! And by comparing one with the other how easy it is to gauge the difference between a commonplace style and nobility of form.

The other writers of the ante-Nicene period nearly all appear as *literati*; Minucius Felix, the graceful writer of *Octavius*; Arnobius, the slightly affected Apologist of the *Adversus Nationes;* Lactantius, who has sometimes been called the Christian Cicero, and others, whose names and works we shall meet with later. May we not even add that there are none, even to Commodianus, who did not endeavour to rise above the commonplace by translating their daily experiences into verse? Commodianus is a poor poet, and scholars still ask themselves what was his strange method; nevertheless he was the first among Christians to conceive and realize a poetry apart from hymns and liturgical compositions. His good will is more touching than a striking success.

Nor must we think that these literary Christians were merely amusing themselves with their own skill,

## THE FIRST SIX CENTURIES

or that they wrote with no other motive than the pleasure of arranging words and phrases. On the contrary they were exceedingly serious and regarded their labour as writers in the light of the accomplishment of a religious task. Whether as priests, like Tertullian and Novatian, bishops, like S. Cyprian, or simple laymen like Minucius Felix, Arnobius and Lactantius, they all display an equal anxiety to serve and defend the Church. They write well, because, before their conversion, they had studied under the best masters of profane learning, even if they had not themselves exercised the office of rhetor, and when they became Christians they did not feel obliged to be false to their early formation. But this was a detail: the essential for them was to set forth their faith, to combat heresy and encourage their brethren. One can better understand the gravity with which they regarded their mission if we compare them with the pagan writers of the same period: Fronto, the tutor of Marcus Aurelius, who wrote sentimentally in praise of smoke, dust and negligence, and who carried his simplicity or his pride so far as to be grieved when his pupil turned from such futile exercises; Apuleius, the elegant narrator of the *Metamorphoses*, for whom the highest art consisted in the carving of empty phrases; or the compilers of the *August History*, where the chief work is the fabrication of their heroes' imaginary discourses and letters. Whilst pagan literature is foundering in an empty and tiresome pedantry, the Christian writers alone claim our attention, because they alone have something to say.

These writers show themselves to be thoroughly Latin by their intense preoccupation with the practical side of life. They leave to the Greeks the interest of the great doctrinal questions; not only to the Oriental Greeks, but even, up to the middle of the third century, to those domiciled in the West. S. Irenæus wrote a great work, *Adversus Hæreses*, where, not content with refuting Gnosticism, he recalls the traditional teaching of the Church on God, the soul and the universe: the writings of S. Hippolytus are very multifarious in character; he occupied himself in turn with exegesis, liturgy, chronology, defence against heresies, and in addition dreamt of imposing a theology of his own on the Church. Tertullian, who was the contemporary of both these men, treats particularly of prayer, baptism, penance and purity; he is interested in the veil and mantle of women, as well as in their jewels, in the theatre, fasting and second marriages; if he contends with Marcion, Valentinian, Hermogenes or Praxeas, it is because the theories of all these heretics affect the lives of the faithful, and when he composes his *Apologeticus* he writes as a jurist rather than a philosopher.

It would be as dangerous to exaggerate this opposition between the Greek and Latin spirit as it would be vain to deny it. Christianity did not create it; she found it ready made, inherent, as it were, in the nature of things, and she profited by it. For these writers portray in strong relief the seriousness of life, and they promulgate the rule of morals, sometimes, like Tertullian, with rash exaggeration, but more often, like S. Cyprian, with prudent and moderate gravity; and always with a beautiful respect.

When the Edict of Milan gave peace to the Church, Christian literature seemed at first, more

## THE FIRST SIX CENTURIES

particularly in the West, to come to a standstill. There is scarcely any name worthy of mention before the year 350. It is useless to try and explain this sterility. Possibly there is no other reason than the peace itself, both within and without, and the disappearance of those agonizing problems, which, in the preceding periods, had provoked such eloquent replies. At any rate it is certain that it was not until Arianism began to be a danger to the Western world, under the reign of Constantius, that any great writers arose in defence of the Faith. S. Hilary of Poitiers appeared, together with SS. Phœbadius of Agen, Eusebius of Vercelli, Lucifer of Cagliari and some others, during the heroic period of the great struggles. He and his contemporaries wrote chiefly to combat heresy and expound the Christian doctrine, and they did this with very different and sometimes opposite temperaments—and, it must be added, with greatly differing success. S. Hilary is the only writer who shows real talent; the rest have nothing in common with him save their orthodoxy and their great zeal against Arianism.

S. Ambrose ascended the episcopal throne of Milan on the eve of the Church's decisive victories; his firmness assured the triumph of the Catholic cause; his perfect knowledge of men and things enabled him later to exercise a preponderating influence on the gravest affairs of State under Gratian, Valentinian and Theodosius. Next to S. Augustine he is the model of bishops.

S. Jerome enters on the scene too late for the combat with Arianism, but he finds many other opportunities for the exercise of his polemical gifts. Helvidius, Jovinian, Rufinus, Vigilantius—to cite only his most illustrious victims—fall one after another beneath the hammer of his pitilessly spiritual blows: so far not one of them has risen again. But S. Jerome possessed many other qualities besides those of a controversialist. His exegetical works have definitely assured his reputation; above all, his translation of the Old Testament from the Hebrew; whilst in his letters we live again in the Roman society of the end of the fourth century.

S. Augustine is numbered amongst S. Jerome's correspondents, thus linking one generation to another. S. Augustine is greater than any of those who preceded him; he is one of the most powerful geniuses that have illustrated the Church—we may even say the whole world. As a writer—and we have chiefly to consider him from this narrow angle —he has handled every subject, and in all has shown himself supreme. A controversialist in his treatises against the Manicheans, Donatists and Pelagians; a theologian in his books on the Trinity; an historian in *The City of God*; a moralist, preacher, letter-writer and philosopher; he is all these and much more. Everywhere and above everything he is himself, the man whose *Confessions* reveal a peerless soul and constitute a work that will remain through the centuries as one of those books over which every reader has wept.

After S. Augustine there begins a new period in the history of literature, as well as in the general history of the Church. The barbarians invaded the Empire of the West and little by little established their kingdoms on the ruins of the Roman power. Less favoured than the East, where classical traditions were preserved for some centuries, the West became the theatre of incessant disturbances, savage

## THE FIRST SIX CENTURIES

wars and multiplied revolutions, and under such tragic conditions it was with difficulty that historians who sought for motives of hope in the lessons of the past, or moralists who endeavoured to explain the austere rules of Christian life to their coarse and savage conquerors were able to write. The language became corrupted by contact with the strange races who introduced into it numbers of new words and incorrect expressions; men of culture grew weary of useless attempts to save from barbarism some vestiges of ancient beauty. The time of great works of art, learned compositions and noble treatises had gone by; urgent needs claimed the zeal of bishops and priests, and even of monks, whose monasteries became the last refuge of a civilization in peril. S. Cæsarius of Arles does not scruple to adapt the sermons of S. Augustine to the needs of his flock rather than compose new homilies, and it required the optimism of a Cassiodorus to venture on publishing the *Institutiones divinarum et sæcularium literarum*, with as much courage as if the world at that barbarous period had leisure to read and work.

It is generally agreed to close the Patristic Period with the name of S. Isidore of Seville, who died in 636. It is needless to remark that his contemporaries noticed no great change after the death of the great bishop, and that the evolution, already long begun, proceeded without shock during the succeeding centuries. But if the historian is obliged to mark stages, and, for the convenience of his work, to interrupt the chain of events, it must be acknowledged that Isidore's name is well chosen to characterize the end of the Age of Antiquity. In fact, the Bishop of Seville's special mission was to

## THE CHRISTIAN LATIN LITERATURE OF

epitomize all human knowledge and to leave to future ages the riches accumulated by the past. His *Etymologies* contain the fruits of the best classic culture, and it is to this book, constantly recopied, that the Middle Ages owed much of their knowledge.

It was, then, during about four and a half centuries, from 180 to 636, that the Christian Latin literature whose history this little book is to trace, developed. We can now see that it is possible to divide this long period into three principal parts. The first, which extends to the Edict of Milan (313), is that of beginnings, when Africa alone gives to the Latin Church writers who are worthy of mention. The second part of our history embraces the whole of the fourth century, down to the death of S. Augustine (430), the period that in the East is the Golden Age of Greek Christian literature. It would be unjust to Tertullian, S. Cyprian and Lactantius to apply this title to the Latin literature of the fourth century, but we may without risk of error describe the period when S. Hilary, S. Ambrose, S. Jerome and S. Augustine were writing as the Age of the Great Doctors. After the death of S. Augustine the struggle with barbarism began, and we see Christian literature doomed to an inevitable decline, only delayed by the talents of a few great minds, who, from S. Leo to S. Gregory the Great and S. Isidore of Seville, form the links of a chain.

Need we add that this history is of immense interest to us? It was for long despised and disdained. It seemed to scholars that Latin civilization had uttered almost its last word before the end of the second century, and that none of the writers after that time deserved the honour of being named. They have now retracted this unjust verdict, and

## THE FIRST SIX CENTURIES

more recent studies of the language of these great Doctors and others prove demonstratively that the Fathers of the Church wrote in a manner not unworthy of Cicero, Cæsar or Tacitus, although they may have employed new expressions and unusual constructions. Grammarians have the right to accept such writers as Cicero and Cæsar as the only authors whose style they would propose for the imitation of their disciples, but historians cannot consent to have their horizons bounded in this way. They ought more especially to study Christian writers because, from the middle of the second century they are the only original thinkers whose message has enriched posterity. If we compare Apuleius with Tertullian, the rhetors of Autun with Lactantius, Symmachus with S. Ambrose, we shall see at once on which side are to be found the greatest minds. And we, the Westerns of the twentieth century, are, perhaps in spite of ourselves, the intellectual and moral heirs of these Fathers of the Church. We have been moulded by the ideas which they first expressed; we have been imbued with sentiments of which they were the preachers. How can we know or understand ourselves if we are ignorant of the source of the current which bears us onwards?

# FIRST PERIOD

## THE BEGINNINGS
(SECOND AND THIRD CENTURIES)

# SUMMARY

UNTIL the Peace of Milan Africa was the only country where a Christian Latin literature developed. At a time when the Church still spoke Greek in Rome and Gaul she was already writing Latin in Africa, and when she finally adopted the vernacular in other countries it was in Africa alone that men were found capable of employing it with distinction for permanent works.

Historical circumstances explain these facts to a certain extent, but they do not suffice to account for such personalities as those of Tertullian and S. Cyprian. It was not, however, a matter of indifference to the later development of Christian thought in the West that its first Latin interpreter should have been Tertullian. He impressed upon it the judicial tone of his reasoning, and in addition created terms which are still used to express the most abstract mysteries: from this point of view a book like the *Adversus Praxean* has an immense importance for the understanding of dogmas. But Tertullian was too independent to remain the faithful disciple of the Church, which could scarcely recognize herself in the fiery rhetorician who breaks every precedent and passes every limit by which he should be bound. The Church much prefers the Bishop of Carthage, always prudent in his actions and just in his judgments, though he too can express himself vigorously on erroneous opinions.

From this first period of its development Christian Latin literature adopted a form that suited it and to which it remained faithful. It was chiefly occupied with practical problems, the relations between Christians and pagans, the duties of the various classes of the faithful and rules of conduct for different states of life. Moral questions had always interested the Romans more than metaphysics, and in this (as has been already said), Tertullian and S. Cyprian showed themselves thoroughly Roman.

At the beginning of the fourth century Arnobius and Lactantius are pure rhetors. The care that they took to compose their Apologies in polished language should be noticed, for at that time no Greek writer showed the same anxiety. They both use literary forms as a means of apostolate; they figure as pupils of Cicero and imitate his style in order to imbue the Christian Church with a literary spirit, and to those who follow them they teach a lesson, the fruits of which will not be lost.

# CHAPTER 1

### THE BEGINNINGS

I. Translations.  II. First Attempts.

THE origin of Christian Latin literature is shrouded in darkness. At what precise moment did Western Christianity begin to write in Latin? In which community were the most ancient formulas drawn up? Who first employed the vulgar tongue in the service of the Christian Faith? Such questions are insoluble, and therefore perhaps out of place. Preachers of the Gospel very early made use of Latin; this was absolutely necessary as soon as they began their endeavours to convert the Romans or Africans who did not know Greek. These converts continued to speak Latin, and, naturally, the inscriptions carved on their tombs were in the same tongue. It is probable that the Catacombs of Rome and Hadrumetum, in North Africa, have thus transmitted to us the earliest monuments of Latin Christianity.

## *I. Translations*

Inscriptions are not, however, strictly speaking, literary works, and can only be cited here by way of record. Christian Latin literature really began with

## THE CHRISTIAN LATIN LITERATURE OF

translations. The Church employed officially the venerable Greek version of the Old Testament, known as the Septuagint, and the Greek New Testament, written in that tongue by its inspired authors. In the course of the second century private persons set themselves to translate at least those portions of the Sacred Books which held an important place in catechetical instructions. S. Augustine, the oldest writer who has mentioned the subject, writes: " We can reckon up the number of those who have translated the Scriptures from Hebrew into Greek, but not the Latin interpreters, for, in the early days of the Faith, all those into whose hands a Greek manuscript might fall, and who thought they knew a little of both languages, had the audacity to make translations." However inexact may be this testimony of S. Augustine, it expresses even to-day the little that we know of the first attempts in the West to translate the Greek Bible. There was no official initiative, but almost everywhere, especially in Rome and Carthage, there were private efforts which resulted in more or less complete versions of the Sacred Text.

In Rome the Marcionites were probably the first to employ Latin translations of the Gospel of S. Luke and the ten Epistles of S. Paul, under the form in which their leader had himself accepted them. The existence of this Marcionite version of the New Testament is clearly attested in the first years of the third century by Tertullian, and it is certain that it could not have been written much later than the year 150, which marks the apogee of the heretical propaganda in Rome.

It is possible that the Roman Catholics very soon produced a complete orthodox translation of the

## THE FIRST SIX CENTURIES

New Testament, in opposition to the heretical one, and that they even translated into Latin the most important Books of the Old Testament. But we have no precise information on this point, and the existence of a *vetus romana*, admitted by some recent historians, cannot be proved with certainty.

We must also confess our ignorance on the subject of the so-called Italian version, the *Itala*, of which certain interpreters profess to find the approval in an obscure text of S. Augustine. Considering the obstinate discussions that have taken place over this text, we cannot, in the absence of all proof, regard the *Itala* as deserving the importance that has been attached to it as a very ancient version.

We are perhaps better informed on the work accomplished in Africa. We know, in fact, that the martyrs of Scillium, put to death for the Faith in 180, possessed " venerable books of the divine law and the Epistles of the just Paul." As these blessed martyrs were simple and unlettered men they could only have possessed Latin translations. We have, indeed, more precise details for the years that followed the death of the Scillitanians in the works of Tertullian. He recurs often enough to the Greek text of the Old and New Testaments, upon which he relies as on an incontestable authority, but he knows and quotes the Latin translations. Whatever may be the liberty with which he cites the expressions of the Sacred Books, there are unequivocal traces of a version—which S. Cyprian used later on—which included at least Genesis, Deuteronomy, the four great Prophets, the Psalms and Proverbs, the Gospels, the chief Epistles of S. Paul and the Acts of the Apostles. This translation without doubt originated in Africa: nothing authorizes us to suppose that it came from Rome, where Greek was still the official language of the Church, and we have every reason to believe that it came from Carthage, where everyone spoke Latin. And it would be imprudent to speak of a unique version. In the middle of the third century S. Cyprian endeavoured by his example and authority to impose upon his colleagues and the faithful a single translation, to the exclusion of all others, and thanks to the many Scriptural quotations in the works of this great bishop, it is possible to reconstruct to some extent the translation that he preferred; but before him there had been many attempts made by non-literary persons.

The Sacred Books were not the only ones to be translated into Latin. Several original Christian works were soon thus translated: the *Letter of S. Clement to the Corinthians*, and at least the first six chapters of the *Doctrine of the Apostles*. The *Pastor* of Hermas existed in Latin before the end of the second century, and we still possess these ancient versions, which testify in their own way the intellectual vitality of the Western communities, particularly that of Rome, for it is probable that the translations of S. Clement's *Letter* and the *Pastor* were made there, both writings being of Roman origin and read there as zealously as in the rest of the Christian world.

We should possess a still more striking testimony to this vitality if we could exactly fix the date of the Latin translation of the *Adversus Hæreses* of S. Irenæus. This great book was written in Greek soon after 180, and many critics hold that almost directly after its appearance it was honoured by a Latin translation, which was used by Tertullian.

## THE FIRST SIX CENTURIES

Unfortunately the discussion still remains open and other savants attribute this version to the end of the fourth or beginning of the fifth century, which detracts greatly from its literary importance.

Should we include in this early literature of translations the lines known as the *Muratorian Fragment*? It seems to be admitted that the fragment was first written in Greek; but the date and place of its origin are still matters of controversy, and we only notice it here on account of the place it holds in the history of the Biblical canon.

The rôle played by translations of the Bible in the formation and development of Christian Latin literature cannot be too much insisted on. For, in the early Church the Bible was not a sealed book, studied only by a few of the initiated; it was the Word of God on which all the faithful were nourished. On it rested the catechism preparatory to baptism; its testimony served as a starting-point to the apologists in their work of convincing pagans and Jews; preachers commented on it in their familiar homilies, and humble souls, like the Christians of Scyllium, carried it about. Its first translators were so deeply convinced of the sacred character of the Greek text that they were careful to follow it word by word and render every shade of its literal meaning. In order to do this they were obliged to transcribe a number of Greek words that had no equivalent in Latin and to change from their original meaning specifically Latin terms, as well as to create whole passages of new expressions and formulas. Thus the most ancient versions of the Bible introduced a fresh vocabulary into the Roman tongue.

Again, these translators were generally ignorant men without literary culture. They spoke the language of the people, intermixed with vulgarisms, careless of the too strict rules of classical syntax, and it was in this rather barbarous language that the Sacred Books were given to the Roman world. For long did men of letters complain, and for centuries they made the inelegance of the Bible a reproach to Christianity. For a time the Church remained indifferent to this grievance; her most learned sons, such as Tertullian and S. Cyprian, did not feel themselves obliged to write with the same freedom as these translators, but they were not ashamed to quote them, and, more or less consciously, they were their debtors.

No Christian could in fact dispense with the terms that served to express his Faith or the deep realities of his spiritual life. It was necessary to speak of baptism, faith, grace, Redemption, etc. The Bible was the treasure whence all could draw, and thus, in spite of their defects, the ancient versions were for many centuries the inspiration of all Christian writers and left clear traces in all their works.

## II. First Attempts

Before the end of the second century, however, there appeared the first original attempts at a Latin literature, if, that is, we can give the name of literature to such poor essays as the Prologues to S. Paul's Epistles, or the Acts of unknown martyrs. But they were a beginning and so deserve to be noticed.

Several of the most ancient manuscripts of the Vulgate contain a collection of Prologues to the

## THE FIRST SIX CENTURIES

Epistles of S. Paul in which many critics see the work of Marcion, or at any rate of a Marcionite of the second century. The exact origin, and even the original language, are an object of discussion, for we only possess the Latin text. It suffices that they were probably Latin compositions to mention them here.

The *Acts* of the martyrs of Scyllium do not provoke so much controversy. On the 17th of July, 180, twelve Christians of that city appeared before the proconsul Vigellius Saturninus, and having confessed their Faith were condemned to die by the sword. The official report of their examination has been preserved; it is a short account, eloquent in its sobriety, written without affectation in the language of the people and is as valuable to the philologist as to the historian.

A little later, in 202-203, some catechumens of Carthage or its neighbourhood, Perpetua, Saturninus, Secundulus, Revocatus, Felicitas, and the Christian, Saturus, were in their turn imprisoned and died for the Faith. Between a Prologue and an Epilogue, probably the work of Tertullian, is placed the account of their passion by Perpetua and Saturus. The whole is of rare beauty; the martyrs were sufficiently educated to be able to describe their sufferings, their visions and their hope with an eloquent simplicity, whilst the portions written by Tertullian are an admirable revelation of the great orator's soul at the moment of his falling into the Montanist error.

Two other names may be cited to complete what we know or think that we know of this period of first attempts; those of Apollonius and Victor, but they are for us no more than names.

## THE CHRISTIAN LATIN LITERATURE OF

We learn from Eusebius' *Ecclesiastical History* of a martyr, Apollonius, who was put to death in Rome under Commodus. Eusebius says that a report of the trial was drawn up and that he had himself inserted " this prayer " in his *Narratives of the Martyrs*. This latter has been lost, but there are some Greek and Armenian texts which may have been inspired by it. Nothing, however, tends to show that Apollonius himself wrote anything. Only Rufinus, in his translation of Eusebius, claims that Apollonius demanded authorization to write and publish his defence, and S. Jerome goes so far as to speak of an *insigne volumen* which the accused had read before the Senate. It is the assertions of S. Jerome and Rufinus that have made a writer, and a Latin writer, of Apollonius, but we see no reason to believe them.

S. Jerome is, on the contrary, far better informed when he describes Pope Victor (189-199) as a Latin writer. Victor was in fact of African origin, and though, according to custom, he used Greek in his correspondence with the Orientals, there is no doubt that he wrote the treatise *On the Question of Easter* in Latin, as well as some smaller works mentioned in S. Jerome's catalogue. But all these are lost, and the hypothesis, formerly received with favour, that Victor was the author of the pseudo-Cyprianic treatise *De Aleatoribus* seems to be indefensible.

It is therefore evident that the best attempts to pierce the darkness that enshrouds the origins of Christian Latin literature have met with very poor results. All that we know for certain is that from the last half of the second century, if not before, the Christians of Rome and Africa undertook the

## THE FIRST SIX CENTURIES

translation of the Sacred Books and some other writings, thus preparing an instrument which was to serve their successors. A certain number of inscriptions, some Acts of the Martyrs and possibly some Marcionite Prologues—these are all the historian knows before the year 190. But the second century was not to close before a bright light had shone over Carthage and the first of the great Christian writers had appeared in the person of Tertullian.

# CHAPTER II

### TERTULLIAN AND MINUCIUS FELIX

I. Tertullian's Life. II. His Works. III. Minucius Felix.

AFRICA was very early evangelized, and there is no doubt that her first apostles, who spoke Greek, addressed themselves in the first place to the Hellenists of Carthage and the coastal towns. But before long the Church of Africa drew most of her members from among the Latins, and by the end of the second century she had adopted the Latin language in preference to Greek, as we see from the example of S. Victor and of Archæus of Septis, who wrote a work on Easter of which we still possess a fragment. It was then that shone forth the powerful talent of Tertullian.

## I. *Life of Tertullian*

Quintus Septimius Florens Tertullianus was born at Carthage in or about 160. His father, a centurion in the proconsular service, and his mother were heathens. Their son grew up in paganism, and by his own account was far from being a model of virtue. But he was an assiduous worker and in the course of his studies assimilated all the knowledge

## THE CHRISTIAN LATIN LITERATURE

of his time. By the time he had reached manhood he wrote and spoke Greek and Latin with equal facility; he had read the best profane authors and had an exact knowledge of the systems of the great philosophers, besides being interested in medicine and the natural sciences. Above all, he had studied law and had absorbed with delight the most abstruse legal theories. He might have become a celebrated rhetor or eminent advocate. But—we hardly know why—he turned a deaf ear to the call of human glory and embraced Christianity.

Having become a Christian he would be a fervent one. His passionate temperament knew no half-measures or hesitations, and as soon as he became a priest he began to preach. He proclaimed his admiration and encouragement to the Confessors under Septimus Severus; to the heathen he showed the injustice of the persecuting laws; against the Jews he proved the fulfilment of prophecy by Jesus Christ. And after having clearly demonstrated the congenital weakness of all heresies, over which the argument of prescription triumphs with ease, he turns against the Valentinians, Hermogenes, Praxeas, and, above all, against Marcion.

But the best of Tertullian's pastoral activity was consecrated to his brethren. He spoke to them of baptism, prayer, patience and penance; he did not disdain to discuss the smallest details of feminine attire; he denounced mixed and second marriages and fulminated against theatres and spectacles. Moral problems interested him particularly, and to each he would offer an absolute and austere solution, often expressed in paradoxical language, which was nevertheless persuasive, and finally, triumphant.

In this way Tertullian exercised his pastoral

ministry for about ten years, from 196 to 206, and
this was the best period of his life. Then, little by
little, he grew embittered; his rancour became more
tenacious, his hatreds more intense and his intran-
sigence more obstinate. No one seemed to him
sufficiently perfect, not only amongst the heathen,
but even among his brethren, and in his sermons,
which he continued with increasing ardour, he
scourged as unpardonable vices the smallest concessions to the exigencies of pagan society.

We know little of the mystery of this development. No doubt it is chiefly explained by Tertullian's
own character; he had always been an enemy of the
golden mean, and even in his youth his temperament
had led him into the worst excesses. His first
Christian works are not exempt from extravagant
assertions, and one feels sometimes that the writer
is doing himself violence not to exceed due limits.
As he grows older he allows himself greater freedom;
his gloomy pessimism increases and his exaggerations pass all bounds. Not having found in the
Church the peace he sought, he condemns the Church
herself, her faithful, her institutions, her indulgence;
he speaks with contempt of the *Psychici* (the
Catholics), who excuse second marriages and allow
a soldier to receive the crown of the *donativum*.
Henceforth nothing stops him on the path of
paradox.

But there was also another cause. External
circumstances certainly favoured Tertullian's change.
All the virtues which this great orator failed to find
in the Church he thought he had discovered amongst
the Montanists—"the disciples of the Paraclete"—
and the partisans of the new prophecy, who seem
to have been pretty numerous at that time in

Carthage. They had attached themselves to a disorderly movement originating in Phrygia about 172, founded by a certain Montanus and two fanatical women, Maximilla and Prisca, or Priscilla. They preached the advent of the Holy Spirit in the person of Montanus, the superiority of free prophecy over the rules of authority, the necessity of corporal renunciation and the condemnation of marriage. Some at least of these theories were already dear to Tertullian, and finding them amongst the Montanists, he thought to find there a port of salvation that Catholicism no longer offered him. Thus, at the end of a continuous development, the beginnings of which can be traced as far back as 206, he broke definitely with the Catholic Church in 212 or 213.

His later works are no more than pamphlets, violent, harsh and paradoxical, but always admirably eloquent, for, in becoming a Montanist Tertullian did not lose any of his natural gifts. Their date remains uncertain and we know nothing of their author's last years. According to a tradition of the fourth century Tertullian did not remain more faithful to the Montanists than he had been to the Catholic Church, but founded a new sect of his own. The members were called Tertullianists, a remnant of whom were reconciled to the Church by S. Augustine. Tertullian died at a great age in the midst of the indifference and forgetfulness of his countrymen.

Posterity has been more generous, and in this has done well, for Tertullian was a great writer. He possessed all the gifts of an orator; a lively imagination, a quick mind and great sensibility. Assisted by his familiarity with profane and Christian literature and a thorough knowledge of law, his trenchant logic shrinks from no objections, but triumphs over every obstacle, though he pushes his theses to the most doubtful extremes in order to manifest his own skill. His style is the image of his thought; strong and vivid, sometimes expanding in harmonious periods, constructed according to the strict rules of rhetoric, more often broken up into short sentences fit to be impressed on the memory and become proverbial. He troubles little about his vocabulary; when a word fails him he coins another, or gives a new meaning to old expressions. The Latin Church owes to him some of her most precious and exact theological terms. Neither does he concern himself much about grammar and syntax; he disregards all rules when they cramp and limit his ardour, and disconcerts the best grammarians, who fail to recognize themselves in the confusion of propositions or the multitude of complements. His manner is certainly not wholly to be praised: he has the defects of his qualities, obscurity, bombast and many others. But it is impossible to read him without being carried away by his impetuous eloquence, and one remains under its charm for long afterwards. Only orators of genius can produce a like impression.

## II. *The Works of Tertullian*

Tertullian enters the domain of literature as an Apologist. After more than half a century of almost uninterrupted publications this kind of literature seemed to be exhausted. The great African renewed it. After having written *To the Martyrs* of the persecution of 197, who seem to

## THE FIRST SIX CENTURIES

have been disputing in their prison, he brought out his first important work, *Ad Nationes*, in two books, which appeared early in 197; then at the end of the same year came the *Apologeticus*. This work is truly unique, for the judicial arguments against the laws of persecution, the satire of heathen religions and the defence of Christian morals unite and display themselves in splendid harmony; some of its pages, masterpieces of eloquence, ring in our memories to this day, whilst many of the formulas have become proverbial. Manuscript tradition bears witness to the popularity of the *Apologeticus*, for it has given us two different recensions, on whose relations one to the other critics are not yet unanimous. The *De Testimonio animæ* (about 200) finishes the series and proves the value of the testimony (to the existence of God and its own immortality) of a naturally Christian soul.

Having thus, in a way, prepared minds for the reception of the Faith, Tertullian addresses himself to the Christians, for one can trace in the series of his works the marks of a regular order. Between 200 and 206 he wrote for the most part treatises of moral instruction, reminding the faithful of the teachings of the Church. Such were the *De oratione; De baptismo; De pænitentia; De patientia.* Three works, *On Fate; On Paradise; On the Hope of the Faithful*, have been lost. He gives his ideas on the theatre in *De spectaculis;* on woman's dress in *De cultu feminarum*, and two books on second marriages in a work that curiously enough are addressed to his wife, *Ad Uxorem.* He refutes the Jews in a treatise, the last chapters of which may not be authentic, and he attacks the Carthaginian painter Hermogenes, the disciple of Marcion, first in a lost treatise, *De censu animæ,* and again in *Adversus Hermogenem,* where he ridicules both the painter and the heretic; also the disciples of Apelles, and Marcion himself (the first edition of this is lost). All these works against the heretics are but the development or the repetition of a work that opposes to all errors the invincible argument of prescription. This little work, *Liber de præscriptione hæreticorum,* has become a classic in the Church; taking prescription in the primitive sense of the word, it demonstrates that heretics have not the right to invoke the testimony of the Scriptures, because these belong exclusively to orthodoxy. Never did Tertullian show himself more solid and stern, and less obscure.

It was about the year 206 that Tertullian began to show his discontent with the Church. The same problems continued to occupy him, but he studied them with increased passion, and it is at this time that he begins to criticize sharply certain concessions accorded by Catholicism. He renews, in a second, and then in a third edition his combat with Marcion, and the result of his efforts was a great work, in five books, filled with texts and information of every kind, which is of immense value for the historical and literary study of the heresy. He attacks the Valentinians, without, however, being able to direct against them anything but a weak compilation of S. Irenæus. He opposes to the Docetism of the Gnostics two works: *De carne Christi* and *De resurrectione Christi.* He explains in a long treatise, *De anima,* his ideas on the soul, its origin, its nature and destiny, and in confirmation of his Stoic materialism declares that a woman has been granted the vision of a soul. Finally he recurs to the moral questions always dear to him, and treats them with ever-increasing harshness. To one of his friends who had become a widower he sends a pressing *Exhortation to chastity;* in *De Virginibus velandis* he measures the correct length of the veil to be worn by virgins; in *De corona*, he inveighs against the weakness of a soldier who should receive the *donativum*, and in a treatise *De idolatriæ* he condemns without remission all Christians who take part in commerce, who are soldiers, schoolmasters or officials; it is the triumph of party spirit. Amongst all these extravagances one is surprised to come upon a strange little book, *De Pallio*, in defence of the philosopher's dress, the *pallium*, which Tertullian had adopted. This witty little composition, written about 206-208, is in strong contrast to his other works of the same period.

The renewal of persecution in 211-12 produced some topical compositions. The *Scorpiace* and *De fuga in Persecutione* forbid the faithful Christian to seek safety in flight, and the letter *Ad Scapulam* again denounces the injustice of persecution. After this Tertullian grows more and more aggressive and reserves his forces to fight against the Church. If he attacks the Monarchian Praxeas it is because he believes the latter had found support in Rome; if he preaches the most absolute *Monogamia*, it is because Catholics allow second marriages; in *De jejunio* he praises the Montanist fasts in opposition to the Catholic practice, whilst a lost treatise, *De ecstasi*, was against the Church's teaching on prophecy. His violence reaches a climax in the treatise *De pudicitia*. It is agreed that this book

—apparently Tertullian's last work—is probably directed against Pope Callistus, but it may possibly have been intended for a bishop of Carthage. It would certainly be impossible to find a more biting irony than is displayed in the invective he discharges on almost every page against the saintly Pope who had decreed that adulterers and fornicators might be absolved after due penance had been done.

Tertullian was an apologist, a theologian, a controversialist and a moralist, and it is difficult to differentiate between the characteristics of his almost exhaustless talent. But if he is to be described in one word it is that of a polemist. His character seemed made for battle; he was not at his ease save when he had adversaries to annihilate, and calm exposition was not his forte. Indeed we see by his extant works that he never practised it, and the titles of his lost writings do not incline us to suppose that he ever improved. Such are *The Vestments of Aaron, The Flesh and the Soul, The Submission of the Soul* and *The Superstition of the World*. But give him opponents and he is instantly ready to pursue and harass them, and then to take the offensive, never relaxing till he has gained the victory.

But whatever may have been his faults, he was an admirable writer, and the influence he has exercised, not only on his immediate successors and on Christian Latin literature, but also in the later centuries, when he has been constantly re-read, is sufficient to class him among the great masters.

# THE FIRST SIX CENTURIES

### III. *Minucius Felix*

The charming and delicate author of *Octavius* was not a great master, like his contemporary, but a refined writer of talent, who understood the power and charm of art; he was, in fact, a classic, and the first Christian classic.

We know little about his life. All that is certain is that Marcus Minucius Felix was born in Africa in the second century and was educated as a pagan; then he went to Rome, where he probably became an advocate, and was converted to Christianity about the same time as his friend Octavius Januarius. The society of the period did not regard such conversions with favour; in the world of letters and philosophy it was considered that Christianity was only fit for the lower and ignorant classes and that men of culture should be content to jest amiably at the Church. A man of education like Felix must often have been called to hold his own in his relations with heathen society and no doubt had many opportunities of refuting the objections that were always in circulation against Christianity. It seemed to him, therefore, that he might render a great service both to the Church and to sceptical heathens by bringing together all the objections and victoriously refuting them. What former apologists had done before emperors, the Senate and the people he would do for a smaller and special public—that most interesting one of *literati*, great wits, friends of eloquence and wisdom. Such a work had never before been attempted, and to succeed required rare qualities of persuasion, vast classical knowledge and a generally elegant distinction. Felix conceived and undertook it, and, what is more, succeeded.

# THE CHRISTIAN LATIN LITERATURE OF

*Octavius*, the title given to this apologetic dialogue, is in its way a small masterpiece. The scene is laid on the seashore at Ostia, which was a favourite resort of the Romans during the summer vacation. Three friends, Octavius, Minucius and Cæcilius, are walking and conversing pleasantly together. The two first are Christians; Cæcilius is still a pagan. They pass a statue of Serapis, and Cæcilius, according to custom, salutes it with a kiss, an incident which directs the conversation to religious subjects. Cæcilius enlarges on his grievances against Christianity and retails all the old objections, those of which the absurdity only provokes the scandalized laughter of the multitude and those preserved in the ancestral traditions of the sceptical worshippers of heathen deities. Cæcilius omits nothing, and his accusations, moderate in tone and cultivated in expression, are all the more solid for the absence of passion. Minucius, who acts as arbitrator, marks the points for discussion, and then Octavius replies. One after another, gravely and calmly, he takes the difficulties expressed by his friend: sometimes a fine touch of irony points his discourse, or a movement of true emotion is apparent, as when he describes the morals of the Christians and the purity of their lives; but he never passes the assigned limits. He does not expect to convert Cæcilius or others like him, but rather to remove their prejudices and show the amiable side of Christianity, so that they may wish it were true, and in this he seems to have succeeded, for at the end of the dialogue the pagan declares himself satisfied and suggests a further discussion on the morrow, to complete his instruction. It is probably because the particular design of this book has not

## THE FIRST SIX CENTURIES

been thoroughly understood that it has been so often debated and even the author's Christianity suspected. Such suspicions lose their force if due attention is paid to the object of the dialogue. The author is satisfied when he has freed the heathen's mind from his prejudices: to ask more of him would be to go beyond his intention.

What makes the *Octavius* so pleasant to read is both the charm of the whole composition and the rare purity of its style. Minucius Felix had been formed in a good school, and he never forgets it. His mind is filled with classic recollections; at almost every moment Cicero, Virgil, Seneca or Tacitus seem to rise up and take the writer's place, but the reader is scarcely conscious of this, so completely are the formulas of the ancient authors assimilated to the thought and style of their imitator. This is certainly not the highest art, and one prefers the tumultuous originality of Tertullian to the tranquil wisdom of Minucius. Still, it is art, and of the best kind.

Tertullian's name cannot be associated with Minucius without raising a grave question concerning the relations between them. Strange resemblances between the *Apologeticus* and *Octavius* have long been noticed, and so strong are they that one of these works must necessarily have been influenced by the other. But so far there is no agreement amongst historians as to whether Tertullian was posterior to Minucius or Minucius to Tertullian. The authorities on either side are equal and the arguments balanced. It is one of those unanswerable questions which seem to exist for the express benefit of critics.

# CHAPTER III

### SAINT CYPRIAN AND HIS CONTEMPORARIES

I. The Writings of Saint Cyprian. II. Novatian. III. Saint Cyprian's Contemporaries. IV. Commodianus.

IN the year 249 the episcopal see of Carthage became vacant by the death of Donatus and a priest of the city named Cæcilius Cyprianus was nominated to it. He began life as a heathen, and after a course of profound study became a teacher of rhetoric and a pleader at the bar of his native city. Neither his daily occupations nor his relations with the cultivated society of Carthage attracted him to Christianity, and his conversion was due to an aged priest named Cæcilianus, with whom he became intimate and who exercised so considerable an influence over his mind that in due course Cyprian received baptism. On his conversion he gave up most of his property to the poor, renounced the prospect of earthly fame, and soon afterwards was ordained priest. This event took place soon after 245, and we can measure what must have been his popularity by the fact that four years later he was elected bishop. Five priests opposed the choice and became his enemies, but S. Cyprian tells us himself that he was " validly elected Bishop, by the voice of the people, the votes of the clergy and the consent of the bishops."

# THE CHRISTIAN LATIN LITERATURE

From that moment Cyprian made himself all to all, and the grave conditions under which he had to exercise his office found him always ready. The persecutions under Decius and Valerian, the schism in his Church, the questions on the treatment of the lapsed, and the baptismal controversy—in which he was certainly betrayed into over strong and heated expressions, but in which he showed his earnest desire to defend the ancient traditions of the Church of Carthage; such were the chief events of his troubled but fruitful episcopate.

After having been exiled by Valerian's first edict he suffered under the increased rigour of the second. He returned to Carthage that he might die in his episcopal city, in the midst of his flock. There he was arrested, judged and beheaded. His martyrdom took place on the 14th of September, 258.

## I. *The Writings of Saint Cyprian*

It was not to be expected that under such circumstances a man like S. Cyprian should ever write merely for his own pleasure. In more peaceful times, perhaps, he might have delighted in culling the flowers of rhetoric, and his earliest work, *Ad Donatum*, in which he relates the marvellous transformation wrought in his soul by divine grace, is written in an affected and bombastic manner, which shows us what he could have done in that line. Literary history has no cause to regret that events caused him to change his style. What is certain is that from the first days of his episcopate Cyprian had a clear understanding of his new responsibilities.

and henceforth all his writings are of a practical character.

Some of these are collections of notes, quotations and arguments put together, perhaps rather hastily, but arranged in a methodical and exact order, so as to be ready at hand when needed. Such is the *Testimonia ad Quirinum*, in three books, which consists of passages from the Old and New Testaments illustrating the passing of the Old Law and its fulfilment in Christ, which Catholics can make use of against pagans and Jews. Another work is *Ad Fortunatum*, grouping together in the same way the Scriptural arguments on the conduct to be observed during the times of persecution. A short treatise, *Quod idola dii non sint*, is oddly composed of extracts, chiefly copied textually from Tertullian and Minucius Felix. It is quite authentic, in spite of the doubts that have sometimes been cast upon it.

The two first of these three works are of very great importance, as illustrating the condition of the Latin Bible in Africa in the middle of the third century. They also manifest the administrative power of their author, for at a time when the numberless translations of the Sacred Books were disputing for ascendancy, S. Cyprian adopts one of these versions, to which he remains deliberately faithful, thus bringing order out of chaos.

His other writings are pastoral instructions and letters, to teach and strengthen the faithful. In one, *Ad Demetrianum*, the Bishop proves, not without some pungent irony, that Christians are not responsible for the calamities of the world; to the people of Carthage, terrified by the invasion of the plague, he strives to bring calm in the beautiful pamphlet, *On the Mortality*, reminding them of the

## THE FIRST SIX CENTURIES

great truths of human destiny. He instructs his flock on all the essential points of Christian life in such treatises as those *On the Lord's Prayer; On the Dress proper to consecrated Virgins; On Almsgiving; On Patience; On Rivalry and Jealousy.* The titles of these works warn us not to seek in them much originality. The same subjects had been treated by Tertullian, but S. Cyprian, while borrowing from him whom he is said to have loved to speak of as " the Master," gives a practical character to these subjects, and a reasonable tone that we vainly seek in the harsh African. The Bishop realizes that he has the charge of souls and the weight of a great responsibility, and his tone is always that of a pastor.

Two of the Saints' works deserve separate mention, as being of special importance: the treatises *De Lapsi,* and *De Ecclesiæ Catholicæ Unitate.* Both were read in the council of 251, and from the circumstances which gave rise to them are of peculiar gravity. After the persecution of Decius many of those who had lapsed through fear begged to be reconciled to the Church, and some imprudent confessors were in too great haste to comply with their request. The Bishop, though showing himself ready to pardon, insisted that the guilty must first be subjected to due penance. On the other hand certain rebellious priests accused Cyprian of having fled during the persecution, and even fomented a schism against him. It was in reference to this rebellion that the Bishop wrote his energetic declaration on the Unity of the Catholic Church, where he demonstrates in admirable words that there can only be one bishop in a Church and one Church in a diocese. It was easy to extend this thesis to the

Catholic Church as a whole, and some controversialists have not failed thus to interpret S. Cyprian's book: possibly the Bishop may have been willing to give it this wider interpretation, if he was really the author of the important interpolations found in some of the manuscripts.

The most remarkable portions of Cyprian's literary work are his letters. Sixty-five of these have been preserved, spread unequally over the nine years of his episcopate, but it is known that there were many others that have not yet been found. The Bishop himself made packets of the letters he both wrote and received, so that our collections are those actually put together by himself. In them we can catch the echoes of those great events that troubled Cyprian's time: the situation of the lapsed; the rebellion of Novatus, the schismatic Carthaginian priest, and his deacon, Felicissimus; the affairs of the sees of Astorga, Emerita and Arles; the baptismal controversy. We can assist at the African councils, in whose name many of these letters are written, and even count the votes in the Synod of 256. In these same letters we contemplate the cruel sufferings of the Confessors of the Faith, condemned to prison or thrown into the mines. Above all, we here behold the ever-watchful activity of a great bishop; the ardour of his zeal, his tender charity, the prudent wisdom of his counsels, his energetic claim of an authority that he knows he has received from God alone. And then, towards the end, we read, expressed in terms of deep emotion, of his brave advance towards certain martyrdom. There scarcely exists any correspondence that is more precious than this, revealing as it does the transparently pure soul of the writer.

## THE FIRST SIX CENTURIES

Although he only took up his pen to fulfil the obligations of his charge, S. Cyprian was nevertheless a great writer. His literary formation had been very complete, and though he never quotes heathen authors, his writings are full of reminiscences of Cicero and Virgil. He is much more classical than Tertullian, not only because he is more reasonable and moderate, but also because he attains without effort a greater perfection in the grouping of words and the harmony of sounds; his phrases generally develop into long periods, with the construction of which not the most exacting stylist can find fault. Perhaps, had he been able to follow his bent he would have left us some elegant and useless compositions in the common fashion of rhetoric; but as a Christian and a bishop he takes his literary work seriously, and writes without affectation or preciosity.

With the exception of the Bible, which he knows thoroughly and constantly quotes, and Tertullian, by whom he was greatly influenced, he does not seem to have known any Christian books; his ideas are his own, born of his experience and reflection, which is shown by the earnestness with which he develops them. All these qualities make of S. Cyprian a Christian classic: less original than Tertullian, less elegant than Minucius Felix, he appears to us more simply human, and this was perhaps why, even in his own time, he was often imitated.

One only borrows from the rich. S. Cyprian's name has been given to many books, the real origin of which it is difficult to determine. Some African writings reflecting his ideas certainly belong to his school: *De Laude Martyrii*, written in 252-3, sometimes attributed to the deacon, Pontius; an *Exhorta-*

*tion to Penance*, a collection of Biblical quotations analogous to the *Testimonia ad Quirinum*; the homily, *De Aleatoribus*, already mentioned as attributed to Pope Victor, but which seems more probably to have been written in Africa, after 250, by a bishop who had more good intentions than knowledge. There is also another African treatise, *De Rebaptismate*, composed by an opponent of Cyprian and an upholder of the Roman teaching, which is important on account of its theological position.

Other works of the same period, in which some historians find no decisive proofs of an African origin, have been still more disputed. Such in particular are *De singularitate clericorum*, a fervent exhortation to chastity, that has sometimes been attributed to a Donatist bishop of the fourth century, but of which Pope Lucius (250) was more probably the author; a short treatise, *Adversus Judæos*; and a pamphlet, *Ad Novatianum*, which may have been the work of Pope Sixtus II. Finally, two writings, *De Spectaculis* and *De bono Pudicitiæ*, both imitations of Tertullian and bearing some marks of being the work of Novatian.

## II. *Novatian*

It is doubtful whether the two above-mentioned works should be attributed to Novatian. But we know enough of this writer through his life and other certainly authentic books to notice him here.

Novatian belonged to the Roman clergy, amongst whom he was ordained during the persecution of Decius, and, as an austere and learned man, he held

## THE FIRST SIX CENTURIES

a conspicuous position in the community after the martyrdom of S. Fabian, the more so that the Pontifical throne remained vacant for a considerable time. He was twice charged by his colleagues to write in their name to S. Cyprian, on the doctrine of the Roman Church regarding the reconciliation of the lapsed, and these letters still exist amongst the Bishop's correspondence (*Epist.* 30 and 36). They are gracefully expressed and redolent of the high dignity of the Mother Church. At this time Novatian perhaps expected to be made Pope, but when the election became possible Cornelius was chosen. Disappointed in his ambition, Novatian did not hesitate to separate himself from the lawful pastor, under pretence of safeguarding the austerity of the primitive rule. He made himself anti-pope and had numerous followers, and the partisans of his schism engaged the attention of orthodox apologists for a long time.

According to S. Jerome Novatian wrote a great deal: *On Easter; On the Sabbath; On Circumcision, On the Priest; On Prayer; On Jewish Aliments* (*De cibis Judaicis*); *On Persecution* (*De instantia*). This list shows the anti-Jewish polemic of Novatian, which may surprise us, but cannot be explained, as with the exception of the one on Jewish foods, all these treatises are lost. But we still possess Novatian's masterpiece, *De Trinitate*, written, apparently, before the schism, which is the most ancient general exposition of the Christian doctrine on God. The writer expresses himself in firm and masterly terms: whilst relying chiefly on the Sacred Scriptures, he makes no secret of his philosophical leanings and special knowledge of the Stoic School. Later on his teaching, which was certainly incomplete, was regarded as the expression of the Arian error, but the author who saw such a likeness was badly informed. For his period Novatian rendered service to the Church by refuting the Adoptionist and Patripassianist theories that were still being circulated. [Cardinal Newman says that "Novatian approaches more nearly to doctrinal precision than any of the writers of the East and West."]

### III. *The Contemporaries of Saint Cyprian*

Amongst S. Cyprian's correspondence are to be found two letters of Pope Cornelius, who had been opposed by Novatian (*Epist.* 45 and 50), both relating to the schism, and we know of the existence of at least five others on the same subject, also addressed to the Bishop of Carthage. Besides these it is certain that Cornelius wrote three letters to Fabius of Antioch and one to S. Dionysius of Alexandria. These last epistles were certainly written in Greek and show that in the middle of the third century the Roman Church employed either Latin or Greek, according to circumstances, in her official correspondence.

The successors of S. Cornelius, SS. Lucius, Stephen, Sixtus and Dionysius are also known as letter-writers, but there are only extant a Latin fragment on the validity of heretical baptism by S. Stephen, and one in Greek of S. Dionysius on Sabellianism. The only literary interest of these very short extracts is in the testimony they furnish to the bilinguism of the Roman Chancery.

Before Novatian took up his pen to write to S. Cyprian the clergy of Rome had had recourse for the same end to the skill of a very ignorant scribe, whose letter (*Epist.* 8 in Cyprian's collection), written in vulgar Latin, is a very curious linguistic document. In its form it may be likened to the letters of Celerinus and Lucian (21 and 22); of the Confessors of Carthage to S. Cyprian (23); of Caledonius to Cyprian (24); and those of the Confessors of Rome (31), all of which swarm with grammatical errors.

We may now return to Africa, but after the death of S. Cyprian there are few writers or works to be noticed. The martyrdom of the great bishop, so noble in its simplicity, at once became the object of an account taken, if not from official reports, at least from the recollections and notes of eye-witnesses. *The Proconsular Acts* of Cyprian are one of the most precious documents of hagiographical literature. Pontius, one of the Saint's deacons, desired to render homage, in his turn, to his revered bishop, and therefore drew up a biography, poor enough in precise information, but correctly written; the first specimen of a kind that was to become popular.

To the same Pontius has been ascribed, without very strong reasons, *The Passion of SS. Marianus and Jacobus*, and *The Passion of SS. Montanus and Lucius*, four Africans martyred under Valerian. Whoever may have been their author, these accounts have great historical value, and show much literary care.

After these Acts of the Martyrs there only remains to be mentioned a curious document of allegorical exegesis, *De Montibus Sina et Sion*, which rests on S. Cyprian's book, *On Almsgiving*, and must have been the work of a Christian as badly instructed in doctrinal questions as in classical culture. Another work, *On the three Fruits of Human Life*, was only published in 1914. This completes the list of literary productions belonging to 250 and the following years.

## IV. *Commodianus*

The above list would be in fact quite exhaustive were it not allowable to attribute to this period the mysterious personality of Commodianus of Gaza, the author of the two oldest known poems of Latin Christianity, the *Instructiones* and the *Carmen Apologeticum*. Commodianus is not mentioned by S. Jerome nor by any other writer before Genadius, who seems to have known him only through his works. Such a silence is perplexing, and the perplexity is increased on reading his poems. The first is in two books, and consists of eighty essays, of very unequal length, but all composed in the peculiar form of acrostics. Under this rather affected guise of witty trifling very grave questions are treated; apologetics against the Jews and pagans and disciplinary instructions for careless Christians. The second poem is a rather naïve résumé of Christian doctrine; it concludes, as is fitting, with a description of the end of the world, and Millenarian dreams hold a conspicuous place.

Commodianus was certainly a man of the people. He knows neither how to write nor compose, and one asks by what whim he took it into his head to write verse. Nature had richly endowed him; he is intelligent, with an eye for the picturesque, for characteristic details or for a smart hit, and he has a keen sensibility, which sometimes rises into

## THE FIRST SIX CENTURIES

eloquence. With all this he is generous, disinterested, indifferent alike to praise or blame, free of speech and fearless in reproving on occasion the powerful ones of the world. Instinctively one loves and reads him with pleasure, the *Instructiones* in particular, which are richer and more varied, full of realistic pictures of the different classes in Christian society, and biting satires on heathen superstitions. But what a style! His verse may be said to contain the finest collection of barbarisms that could be invented by the worst of Latinists. This is not an exaggerated judgment, for in every line one is arrested by a grammarian's scruple. We silence the criticism and pass on, but however defective may be the transcribed manuscript or the faults of our present editions, Commodianus alone is responsible for his language, which can hardly be described even as the Latin of the people.

He is still more responsible for his versification, for verses are not a mere accidental trick of the scribe. The acrostics of the *Instructiones* show that they are deliberate, and the alliterations, rhymes and assonances prove this. But the verses are so strange that they have disconcerted the cleverest authorities on metre. The deliberate use of some complex system has been suspected, but the reality is quite otherwise. Commodianus, though unacquainted with prosody, tries to write in dactylic hexameter, according to the classical models. Every now and then he succeeds: in the 1066 verses of the *Carmen* there are 26 correct ones. That he has not been more successful is owing to his want of education, his clumsiness, or, perhaps, his carelessness. He finds it enough that the last two feet of his verse should be a dactyl and spondee according to the rules of prosody; the rest does not concern him, and in this he is like the many writers of inscriptions, who, with him, have no sense of measure. It is therefore useless to seek in Commodianus the origin of a new art of versification. Rather do we behold the decline of ancient art.

The impossibility of fixing the date and status of Commodianus is very provoking. In the last acrostic of the *Instructiones*, called *Nomen Gasaei*, he represents himself as *Mendicus Christi*, but this vague title enlightens us no more than does the word *Gasaeus*, in which it is impossible to see any allusion to the Palestinian town of Gaza. Historians have consequently suggested very different hypotheses in explanation of the mystery. Some hold that Commodianus lived in the middle of the fifth century, from 458-466: he would then be a layman in the south of Gaul and his work would be full of allusions to the barbarian invasions and the pontificate of S. Leo. Others assign him to the beginning of the fourth century and make him a compatriot and contemporary of Lactantius, by whose works he was influenced; others again consider that the years 250-258 agree better with the descriptions in the two poems, and that the writer chose to announce the approaching end of the world whilst S. Cyprian was exhorting the faithful not to fall away. This last opinion seems the most probable, and one likes to think that in that troubled period of persecutions, schisms and plague the Christians of Carthage were upheld in their Faith and Hope by two men so utterly different as the Bishop of Carthage and the popular poet, but who were closely united in their common love of the Church of God.

## CHAPTER IV

### THE DAWN OF THE FOURTH CENTURY

I. Arnobius.  II. Lactantius.  III. Reticius and Victorinus.

THE last forty years of the third century display a lamentable void in the history of Christian Latin literature. During this long period there is the name of neither writer nor work deserving of mention; there seems to be a complete sterility. Instead, however, of trying to explain this apparent barrenness, we must remember that we know scarcely anything of the life of the Church during these forty years. The historian, Eusebius, our best and almost only source of information, contents himself with a rapid sketch, in which he gives us a glimpse of the progress of Christianity during the blessing of a long peace, and S. Jerome himself, in spite of his desire to lengthen the catalogue of illustrious writers from whom he could make an Apologetical argument, knows nothing of a period in which, all the same, something must have happened.

When, in 295, the darkness began to grow less, it is in Africa, on occasion of the persecutions, that the first documents worthy of note are to be found. The *Acts* of the conscript Maximilianus of Theveste are one of the most curious pieces that Christian antiquity has left us: the authentic report of Maximilianus and his refusal to serve has been there reproduced almost exactly. The *Acts* of the centurion Marcellus, and the registrar, or recorder, Cassian, at Tingis; of the standard-bearer Fabius, at Cæsarea, and of the veteran Tipasius, at Tigava relate to events anterior to 300 and enable us to assist at a regular purgation of the African army: the actual drawing-up of these Acts seems to belong to a more recent epoch.

The Great Persecution gave birth to a copious literature on the *Passions of the Martyrs*. The *Acts* of Crispina of Theveste, of Saturninus, Dativus and their companions at Abitene, of Bishop Felix of Tibiuca, of the Saints Maxima, Donatilla and Secunda at Thuburbo, are gathered from the official reports or notes taken by the spectators. Whatever may be the value of the extant editions, they all bear witness to the care of the African Church to preserve the memory of her martyrs: in scarcely any other part of the Christian world has so much anxiety been shown.

Africa seems, indeed, to be the special country of *procès-verbaux* and archivist's documents. We still possess an imposing series of writings relating to the persecution, and to the origin of the Donatist schism; an official report of the seizure of the Sacred Books in the Church of Cirta (303); a protocol of the Council of Cirta (305); the correspondence of Mensurius of Carthage and Secundus of Tigisi; complaints of the Donatists to the Emperor; letters of Constantine to Anulinus, to Pope Melchiades, and others; reports of the Council of Rome (313), etc. All these documents are of

## THE FIRST SIX CENTURIES

capital importance for the historian, and some of them, written in popular Latin, are no less interesting from a literary point of view.

However, at the beginning of the fourth century, Christian Africa had something better to show than the Acts of the Martyrs and official documents, for she then gave birth to two Apologists who are among the best Christian writers in the Latin tongue, Arnobius and Lactantius.

### I. *Arnobius*

The story of Arnobius is a strange one. In the year 295 or 296 the heathen society of Sicca Veneria in Proconsular Numidia were electrified by the news that Arnobius, the famous rhetorician, had become a Christian. Nothing could be more unexpected, for Arnobius was an earnest worshipper of the ancient gods and a devout follower of their religion, and he had hitherto pursued Christianity with sarcasm and hatred. Why, asked his compatriots, had he suddenly taken to adore what he had formerly burnt? We may ask the same question. He himself declared that he owed the gift of Faith to a dream, but we may believe that there were also other reasons, such as his philosophical reflections and the sight of Christian virtue. In any case his conversion was so sudden as to disquiet the Bishop of Sicca, who doubted whether it might not be a feint. It was necessary, therefore, to test him. Summoned to show proof of his sincerity, Arnobius did not flinch. Under the title of *Adversus Nationes* he drew up a vigorous Apology for Christianity and an orderly condemnation of pagan religions.

## THE CHRISTIAN LATIN LITERATURE OF

Nothing can be more curious than this work, written by a man who had not yet received baptism and who knew almost nothing of the religion to which he was henceforth to consecrate his life. For Arnobius had not time really to study the Bible or the Christian authors before writing; only three or four Scriptural allusions are to be found in the work, and of his predecessors in Apologetics he knows nothing. But what need had he of study to be convinced? Was it not enough to set forth the vanity of idols and to be impressed by the splendour of Christian life? If human reason is too feeble to reach to knowledge of the truth, if Faith is indispensable in the smallest actions of our life, should he not give his whole heart to a religion of authority, that proclaims the blessedness of the little ones and the simple? There is paradox in such an attitude, but Arnobius is not a man to be afraid of paradox. He brings into the Church all the subtle methods he had taught so successfully in his professor's chair: his *Apology* is the work of a perfect rhetorician.

On reading the first pages of his work, which are devoted to the defence of Christianity, one is surprised that they should have satisfied the bishop, for they manifest a truly disconcerting ignorance. Arnobius there holds that the soul is not the work of Almighty God, but of some secondary divinities; and that the Supreme God is indifferent and impassive according to the teaching of the philosophers. He has strange opinions about Christ Himself, and the prodigies that he attributes to Him are too often outrageous exaggerations of the Gospel narrative.

Happily, the rest of the work is more satisfactory. After having shown that Christians are not respon-

## THE FIRST SIX CENTURIES

sible for the evils in the world, Arnobius passes to the offensive and attacks paganism directly, with pitiless satire. Here, at least, he knows what he is talking about. He is familiar with mythology; its mysteries are not inaccessible to him, and the philosophers' books, particularly those of Cornelius Labeo, provide him with most of his arguments. On such ground as this his spirit and irony have free play, and he does not fear to provoke much laughter by his insistence on the immorality of certain heathen legends. The gods of Greece and Rome are demolished by a master-hand in these revengeful pages, and the Christians of Sicca could fully enjoy the triumph gained for them by their new co-religionist.

Arnobius' style is what is to be expected from a professional rhetorician. One of its most striking characteristics is that of emphasis. Everything is enormous, immoderate with this master of fine language, who fears nothing so much as the commonplace. He likes sonorous expressions, grandiloquent words, repetitions, assonances, alliterations, accumulations of epithets, redounding periphrases: all these fine artifices—which smell a little of the lamp—strike the reader and force his attention. Then, too, if we take into account the circumstances of the time that explain certain negligences in syntax and verbal inventions, Arnobius' language is generally correct.

Clearly, if Arnobius had been only a rhetorician his style would soon become insupportable, in spite of the purity of his language. But he is a sincerely convinced Christian, with some of the most precious gifts of the true orator. At the moment of his conversion he gave himself to Christ and the Church without reserve, and in his book we hear as it were the echo of the deep feelings that then moved him. He is certainly not a first-class writer, but he can be re-read without fatigue, and we should not forget that, centuries before Pascal, he formulated, in almost identical terms, the French writer's celebrated " argument of the wager."

## *II. Lactantius*

Very different from Arnobius, both in mind and in his career, is his disciple, Lactantius. Lucius Cœlius (Cæcilius) Firmianus Lactantius was born in Numidia, about 250. After finishing his classical studies he followed for some time the lectures of Arnobius at Sicca and then himself became a professor of rhetoric, in which profession he continued to the end of his life. About 290 he was sufficiently well known to be appointed by Diocletian to the official professorship of Latin rhetoric in Nicomedia. He remained for some time in this distant city, amongst Orientals who despised the language of Cicero, more or less of an exile, in spite of his official position. As a distraction, and also perhaps in order to perfect his style, he took to writing. He had begun this practice whilst still in Africa, where he wrote a treatise entitled *Symposium*, " A Banquet," in imitation of Plato, the vague title of which covered a variety of subjects. Later, he composed a poem in hexameters, called *Hodœporicum*, describing the journey from Africa to his new home. This also was a tribute to the literary fashion of the time. To these first writings succeeded others which we know from S. Jerome: a *Grammaticus*; two books to Asclepiades; four books of letters to Probus; two to Severus and two to Demetrianus. Pope S. Damasus knew these letters and expressed regret that they dealt only with profane subjects, metrics, geography and philosophy. These were all probably written before the author's conversion.

For Lactantius, like Arnobius, had been brought up a pagan and did not become a Christian till late in life, that is about the year 300. His conversion did not at first hinder his career, but when, in 306, Galerius closed the schools of Nicomedia he lost his chair and had to leave the city for a time. He then passed through some painful years and was reduced to almost absolute poverty. The Edict of Milan changed the face of things, and about 316 Constantine's friendship raised him from penury and he was appointed Latin tutor to the Emperor's son, Crispus. He gave himself wholly to his new work, so much so that we know nothing of his last years and death.

Lactantius composed his best works after his conversion, those at least which have been preserved and have assured his reputation. The earliest of these is a treatise on the Work of God, *De Opificio Dei* (303-4), an Apologetic in favour of Providence as manifested in the marvellous organization of the body and soul of man. The argument was not new and the Stoics, in particular, had made great use of it. Lactantius, however, took it up afresh, and without showing great originality, or even avoiding some puerile exaggerations, composed a graceful and pleasant book, capable of impressing the many pagan sceptics and scoffers who despised Christianity for its ignorance of philosophy. After this comes " The Divine Institutions," in seven books, *Divinarum Institutionum Libri VII*, Lactantius' chief work. The seven books treat successively of false religions, the origin of error and false wisdom, then of the true wisdom and the true religion, of justice, true worship and the life of the blessed. These titles show the grandeur and originality of the treatise. No one had hitherto attempted to treat the religious question from such a lofty standpoint nor had furnished such a complete solution. Lactantius addresses himself chiefly to cultivated pagans: he sees around him a multitude of the ignorant and simple crowding into the churches, but on the other hand he finds that his teaching as a Christian Master is unsuccessful, and the intellectuals turn with contempt from his professorial chair. He suffers intensely at this opposition to the teaching of Christianity and is determined to overcome it. He knows that such minds are sensitive to the charm of fine language and he employs the purest classical style that circumstances permit: his vocabulary, his syntax, the art with which he rounds his periods, the care he takes to complete his phrases according to the strict rules of the *Cursus*—all this is redolent of Cicero. And it is not, on the part of Lactantius, the rhetorician's artifice, but the systematic method of the apologist who knows his work. He understands that the better class of pagans need reasonable arguments, drawn from philosophy rather than from the texts of Scripture, and in this way he demonstrates the deficiencies of profane wisdom and shows how Christianity is the only true wisdom, practising justice and leading to true beatitude. It is needless to remark that all his arguments are not new and that he owes much to the Stoics; nor are all his proofs decisive, and he gives too much credence to the Sibyl and Hermes Trismegistus, whom he

## THE FIRST SIX CENTURIES

quotes with almost as much respect as he does the Bible. Criticism here is easy and the deficiencies in this great project are evident. But it is only just to pay homage to its nobility of purpose, and even to the value of its execution. Lactantius has not the wide outlook of Origen, and one cannot compare the great thinker of Alexandria with the African rhetorician, who, following in the footsteps of the former, has tried to start afresh the work of apologetics. Like all good Latins, Lactantius is chiefly interested in moral questions, and he is at his best when studying the rule of morals. Nevertheless the book of *Divine Institutions* is a great work.

After finishing it he composed a summary called *Epitome Divinarum Institutionum*, briefly resuming the different parts and correcting details, thus serving to clarify the great theses of the larger work. This book is addressed to a certain Pentadius. A smaller work, *De Ira Dei*, develops one of those theses—not the most important, but one that was much discussed in the light-minded circle round Lactantius; namely, whether God, immutable and sovereignly perfect, is subject to passion. Most of the philosophers denied this and jeered at the Sacred Books, which speak so frequently of the wrath of God. Some Christians had been led astray by these theories and sought to interpret such passages of Scripture allegorically. Lactantius, with greater courage, rejects such concessions and undertakes to prove that the anger of God is a perfection, because it serves to manifest His supreme power. There is, perhaps, some sophistry in this reply, but it is none the less remarkable for its calm audacity.

This book is a philosophical dissertation, formulating general principles, but Lactantius afterwards wrote a treatise showing the practical consequences of God's anger. In *De Mortibus Persecutorum* we meet with such an unfamiliar tone that the authenticity of the work has been sometimes doubted. But such doubts are without foundation. It was certainly the true Lactantius who, on the morrow of the Peace of Milan, in the exaltation of triumph, drew up this pamphlet, breathing a powerful spirit of satisfied justice. He there proves that God always finally punishes those who persecute His Church. After briefly recalling the history of the first enemies of Christianity, he describes at length the tragic deaths of more recent persecutors. He relates the events he had himself beheld in Nicomedia and those which he has heard from other eye-witnesses; he cites authentic documents, and his work, full of first-hand information, is of real historical value.

One must not, however, forget that Lactantius himself had suffered too much to be strictly impartial. He nourished a fierce hatred against Diocletian and his associates which is constantly apparent and injures the sanity of his judgment. Then, too, he is more anxious to prove a thesis than to write an historical account. But his rhetorical gifts are wonderfully intensified by his personal feelings, and it is just the expression of these that makes the writing so extraordinarily vivid.

That a learned professor so unfit for any kind of action that he had never ventured to exchange his lector's chair for the Bar, should become capable of composing such a violent work as *De Mortibus Persecutorum* could only be the result of quite extraordinary events: the advent of Constantine, the

## THE FIRST SIX CENTURIES

Peace of Milan and the triumph of the Church. When he is not thus raised out of himself by exterior circumstances Lactantius generally writes well; his correct language, his graceful and purely classical phrases betray the effort of a careful stylist. We might prefer a little more spontaneity and freedom. But it is only just to say that though, taken altogether, his talent was not above the ordinary, he understood the task he had set himself and accomplished it with honour. In order to convert the intellectuals of his time he spoke their language and utilized the principles of their philosophy. A more highly endowed man might not have attained his end more perfectly than did this conscientious and methodical rhetorician.

### III. *Reticius and Victorinus*

Outside Africa Christian Latin literature is only represented by two names: one from Gaul, Reticius, Bishop of Autun, the other from Pannonia, Victorinus, Bishop of Pettau. The Christians of these two countries had begun by speaking Greek, and it was in that language that the *Acts* of the Pannonian martyrs, SS. Irenæus and Dasius, were written. They suffered during the Great Persecution, and it was after that time that the majority of the Christians in that region became Latinized. Reticius of Autun is only known as a writer through S. Jerome, and some quotations in S. Augustine. The first attributes to him a large volume, *Against Novatian*, and a *Commentary on the Canticle of Canticles*. Without making much account of the originality of the attempt—Reticius is perhaps the most ancient Western commentator on the Canticle—S. Jerome is very severe on his obscure and affected style: S. Augustine only quotes a few sentences on the baptism of heretics. Neither tell us anything of his work as a bishop, which must have been important, as we know that he was active in the Councils of Rome (313) and Arles (314), in connection with the Donatist heresy.

We are somewhat better informed as to S. Victorinus, Bishop of Pettau, in Styria, martyred under Diocletian. Though a Greek by birth, Victorinus wrote by preference in Latin, but without elegance or harmony, and his language did not find favour with the exacting S. Jerome. His chief works were devoted to the explanation of Scripture and he wrote Commentaries on the Pentateuch, Ecclesiastes, the Canticle, Isaias, Ezechiel, Habacuc, the Gospel of S. Matthew and the Apocalypse. Most of these badly written works soon disappeared; the Commentary on the Apocalypse alone remained popular, in spite of the Millenarian interpretations adopted by the writer. This book was copied, corrected and transposed so many times that it is difficult now to discover the authentic work of Victorinus in these various recensions that are attributed to him.

A little treatise on the Creation of the World, *De Fabrica Mundi*, may belong to him, though antiquity has given it no title. As for the small work, *Against all Heresies*, mentioned by S. Jerome, some have supposed it to be identical with the few pages bearing the same title affixed to Tertullian's *De Præscriptione*, but the hypothesis is more ingenious than probable.

Altogether, these two first representatives of

## THE FIRST SIX CENTURIES

Christian Latin literature in Gaul and Pannonia are more to be respected than admired. Both were bishops and obliged to write by the necessities of their office, which they did without great talent. The almost complete disappearance of their works prevents our expressing any opinion on them, but the severe strictures of S. Jerome probably corresponded with the facts.

# SECOND PERIOD
## THE APOGEE
(313-430)

## SUMMARY

The fourth century is the age of the great Doctors, in the West as well as in the East. It would seem as if all things conspired to make this a specially privileged period. The Church, so long tried by persecution, has received official recognition from the State. The higher classes of society, until now in rebellion against the Church, are being gradually converted, and adorn the religion of Christ with the splendours of intellect and knowledge so ardently desired by Lactantius. The Empire itself, soon to be crushed by the Barbarians, enjoys for the last time the blessings of peace, and, under the rule of a few superior men, presents an illusory picture of eternal stability. No doubt there are many shadows beside the sunshine. The saddest for Christianity are those cast by heresy and schism. But the West is not troubled like the East by the heat of the Arian controversies: it was not till about 355 that the Western Church had to take part in the discussions that for thirty years had disturbed and divided the Church of the East. Even then the former is not greatly troubled by a tempest which is immediately calmed on the death of Constantius II. The Donatist schism does not extend beyond Africa, so that Italy, Gaul and Spain enjoy almost uninterrupted tranquillity.

# THE CHRISTIAN LATIN LITERATURE

The literature accords with the conditions of its development. Controversial in Africa throughout the fourth century, owing to the Donatist schism, elsewhere it is calm. It is employed to teach, exhort and direct, and moral questions are uppermost in the minds of its representatives. There are some great names amongst them, round whom are grouped those of friends and disciples. SS. Hilary, Ambrose, Jerome and Augustine surpass all their contemporaries, and by their virtue and knowledge exert an immense influence on the Catholic Church. The whole world is their country: S. Hilary is exiled to the East, S. Jerome settles in Bethlehem, S. Ambrose and S. Augustine, who remain in the West, have constant intellectual relations with the East, corresponding with those who live there and reading their works. One can hardly assert that one is African and the other Italian: they are both essentially Roman.

The grand figure of S. Augustine dominates the whole period, though his appearance does but mark its conclusion. The Bishop of Hippo possesses such qualities, both of head and heart; he realizes so completely the highest ideal of human nature, that he towers above all those with whom one would compare him. It may be said that in some sort the Roman world terminates with him. After his death the Barbarians can finish their work of destruction.

## CHAPTER V

### SCHISMS AND HERESIES

I. Donatism.  II. Arianism.  III. Victorinus.  IV. Lucifer.
V. Saint Hilary.

WITH the Edict of Milan a new period begins, both for the history of the Church and that of Christian literature. Some of the more ancient kinds are no longer cultivated: why, for example, write *Apologies* now that Christianity has triumphed? The heathen are less and less to be feared as the years pass on, and it is very rare that men like Firmicus Maternus demand their destruction by the emperor. The true enemies of Catholic orthodoxy are the schismatics and heretics who tear the unity of the Church, and it is against them that are multiplied, on the Catholic side, doctrinal treatises, homilies and historical works, whilst the heretics themselves employ similar arms to prove the solid foundation of their pretensions. The greater part of Christian Latin literature, down to about 390, is controversial, in Africa against Donatism, in Italy, Illyria and Gaul with Arianism.

### *I. Donatism*

The Donatist schism broke out at Carthage on the morrow of the Great Persecution. It arose from

## THE CHRISTIAN LATIN LITERATURE OF

apparently trifling causes; rivalry of candidates for the episcopal see of Carthage and discussions on the validity of orders conferred by *traditors* [those who had given up the Holy Scriptures or sacred vessels during the persecution], but very soon passions were inflamed, and under the pretext of religion the old rivalries between Proconsular Africa and the powerful Numidians reappeared. The schism was definitely consummated in 312; the attempts at reunion made in the Councils of Rome (313) and Arles (314) failed, and for a hundred years the Donatist schism was the chief anxiety of African Christianity.

The Donatists soon learned the importance of books and written works: their controversial literature, which was rich and varied from the beginning, developed during the course of the fourth century into an imposing series of letters, sermons, treatises, pamphlets, historical accounts and official documents. Every sort of literature is represented, and though most of these writings are lost, we can gain from extracts in the works of their opponents some idea of the activity of the Donatists in creating a literature of their own.

Donatus of Carthage, the organizer of the schismatical Church, was the first to set an example. He multiplied sermons and treatises; he wrote particularly *On Baptism* and *On the Holy Spirit*; he preached panegyrics on the " martyrs " of his sect; he wrote letters, he spoke in councils; up to the year 347 he pursued his task with untiring zeal. His disciples continued his work: to Vitellius Afer, who wrote during the reign of Constans, are attributed an Apology, *Against the Pagans*, a book, *Against the Traditors*, and another to show *That the Servants of God are hated by the World*. A Petition to the

## THE FIRST SIX CENTURIES

Emperor Julian is supposed to have been by Pontius, and Macrobius, the Donatist bishop in Rome, is thought to be the author of *The Passion* of the Donatist "martyrs," Maximian and Isaac in 347; Gennadius also attributes to him a work entitled *To Confessors and Virgins,* which has been mistakenly confused with the pseudo-Cyprianic treatise *De Singularitate Clericorum.* Later, Parmenianus of Carthage distinguished himself as a leader. He composed a great work in five books, *Against the Church of the Traditors,* which was refuted by S. Optatus, and a *Letter to Tyconius,* which S. Augustine answered. Primianus, his successor, was only an awkward and violent orator; but Petilianus of Constantine, the author of two letters to S. Augustine and of three treatises, *On the Schism of the Maximianists, On the Succession of the Donatist Church* and *On the Only Baptism,* is a writer of merit. The same may be said of Cresconius the grammarian, who addressed a celebrated letter to S. Augustine; of Emeritus of Cæsarea, Gaudentius of Thamugadi and Fulgentius, of whom we have an opusculum *On Baptism.*

Other names might be cited, with anonymous works to complete the list: Donatist editions of authentic Acts of Catholic martyrs, as well as of their own, so-called; Donatist recensions of the works of S. Cyprian; pamphlets and treatises of which traces are found in S. Augustine's refutations. There is little variety of tone or matter in all these, only constant repetitions of the same grievances against the Catholic Church, "the Church of the Traditors" as they call it, the same justification of schism, and everywhere the same strained and declamatory style, extravagant and insulting language. The Donatist literature is certainly not wanting in spirit, and its writers are sometimes eloquent in their passionate belief, but they are all much alike and their monotony becomes wearisome.

The only writer of the sect who deserves separate mention, on account both of his independence and the moderation of his style, is Tyconius, or Tichonius. This cultivated and prudent layman was, it seems, a seeker after truth, and was not content with the teaching of the bishops of his party. He wishes to discover for himself the ground of their assertions, and with this intention he studies the Bible carefully, traces the original causes of the schism and discusses the arguments and proofs. He often decides against the Donatist Church, and one then expects to find him returning to orthodox Catholicity. But with a strange want of logic he remains where he is, in spite of the suspicions of his own hierarchy. He expounds his ideas in *The Intestine War* (370) and in the *Expositiones diversarum causarum* (about 375), of which Parmenianus wrote a refutation. A little later he wrote a *Commentary on the Apocalypse* which was many times used by later exegetists and is supposed to be almost completely extant in the commentary of Beatus of Libana. Finally, about 382, he composed the most celebrated of his works, *De Septem Regulis*, in which he claims to provide interpreters of Scripture with a sure and easy means of explaining all the obscure texts of the Bible. These rules of Tyconius were inserted by S. Augustine in his *De Doctrina Christiana* and were afterwards often copied. Tyconius is an estimable writer, full of sympathy and broadmindedness, whose clear and correct style fixes the reader's attention.

## THE FIRST SIX CENTURIES

There is naturally an Antidonatist literature opposed to that of the sect, but it is less rich and vivid. It would seem that the Catholics were long in realizing the necessity of defending their position or taking the offensive. At first they were content with preserving the early documents of the controversy, the *Gesta purgationis Cæciliani et Felicis*, the episcopal and imperial letters and Conciliar Acts, but they did not make use of these documents which nevertheless bring out so clearly the original fault of the schismatics.

It was only in the middle of the fourth century that they found a capable defender in the person of S. Optatus, Bishop of Milevis in Numidia. Parmenianus' work, drawn up on his return to Africa (362), was having a great success among the Donatists and was troubling the consciences of a good many Catholics, and a refutation became urgent. This refutation appeared in the six books of Optatus, *De Schismate Donatistarum*, completed about 366. To the arguments of the schismatical primate of Carthage the Bishop of Milevis first opposes the facts; he recalls the beginnings of the schism and its subsequent history; he insists on the results of the Edict of Union in 347 and the deaths of the pretended Donatist martyrs. Then he shows clearly the Notes of the true Church and the injustice of the claims of his opponents to the sole possession of true sanctity. It is all clearly and frankly expressed: Optatus there manifests the true qualities of the historian, and in his theological arguments betrays a shrewd intellect and an exact comprehension of doctrine. His style is certainly sometimes over-emphatic and grandiloquent, a common defect with all Africans. The permanent success of his work is evidence of its necessity: twenty years later he was obliged to bring out a new edition, augmented by a seventh book, in which he replies to certain objections. It is possible that death surprised him in the midst of his labours, for this seventh book seems to be unfinished. Until within the last few years Optatus was only known by this controversial work; now there has been a fortunate discovery of a sermon of his for the feast of Christmas, simple and persuasive, as we know the Bishop of Milevis to have been.

Optatus thus gave an example to the Catholics which was followed. After him S. Augustine and his friends entered the lists and strove valiantly against the Donatists; but we shall return to them later on. We must now go back to Europe and assist at the vicissitudes of the combat waged between Arians and Antiarians.

## II. *Arianism*

For a long time Arianism remained almost unknown in the West and only some few persons in positions of authority had been forced to take notice of it. Pope Julius (337-352) had written two remarkable letters to the Orientals and Alexandrians which we possess in the Greek text, and several Latin letters are attributed to Pope Liberius, those to Cæcilianus of Spoleto, Ossius of Cordova, Eusebius of Vercelli, Ursatius of Singidunum and Germinius of Sirmium, to Vincent of Capua, etc., and even a letter in Greek to S. Athanasius, but the authenticity of many of these is disputed. Ossius of Cordova addressed a letter from Sardica to Pope

## THE FIRST SIX CENTURIES

Julius recommending the adoption of a new Symbol and later wrote to the Emperor Constantius to oppose his pretensions. But all this does not take us very far.

It was from Illyricum, especially after the arrival of the Emperor Constantius, that the Westerns became acquainted with Arianism. We possess little besides fragments of this Arian literature, which must have been rich. A letter and profession of Faith are all that remain from Germinius of Sirmium, who figures as one of the interlocutors in the curious *Dispute* of the layman Heraclian with the Bishop of Sirmium on the Faith of the Councils of Nicæa and Rimini.

We know of a few fragments of a treatise by Palladius of Ratiara against the *De Fide* of S. Ambrose. Ulphilas, the celebrated translator of the Bible into Gothic, left numerous sermons and commentaries which have disappeared, and we have only under his name a profession of faith in Latin. Auxentius of Dorostorum is the author of a letter on the faith, life and death of Ulphilas, which seems to have been retouched by Maximus. This last is the only one of the Illyrians of whom we possess much. There is a *Disputatio Maximini contra Ambrosinum*, reproducing a controversy of the Gothic bishop with S. Ambrose, and also an important series of homilies that were for long wrongly attributed to S. Maximus of Turin. We know too that this bishop had a dispute in 420 with S. Augustine, who published an account of the discussion. Some have also attributed to him a commentary on S. Matthew, the famous *Opus Imperfectum* which was thought so much of in the Middle Ages: it is, however, probable that this work is much later than Maximus and dates from the sixth century, being the work of the Latin adapter of the volumes of Origen on S. Matthew. Some fragments of homilies on the Gospel of S. Luke, published by Mai, according to the manuscripts of Bobbio, are anonymous, but seem to have emanated from Illyricum and to date from the end of the fourth century. From all these we gain an insight into the way in which Arian literature developed on the banks of the Danube: it is to be regretted that so little of it has been preserved.

Outside the Illyrian regions Arianism was far from obtaining a like success. The only writers to be mentioned are Potamius of Lisbon, to whom we owe a letter to S. Athanasius (355) and two homilies, on Lazarus and the martyrdom of the prophet Isaias, which show an extraordinary predilection for realistic details; and Candidus, apparently an Italian, who wrote a *Letter* to Victorinus and a treatise on *The Divine Generation*, which was refuted by the same Victorinus.

### III. *Victorinus*

Caius Marius Victorinus (often referred to as Victorinus Afer) was one of the first to attack Arianism. He was born in Proconsular Africa about the year 300 and went to Rome in 340, where he taught rhetoric with immense success. He was then a heathen, and on every occasion riddled the Church and Christian doctrine with his sarcasms. In order to refute Catholicism more efficaciously he began to read the Bible and other Christian literature, with the wholly unexpected result of bringing about his conversion, and towards 355 the famous rhetorician declared himself a Christian.

Before his conversion he had published several works that show great learning and penetration of mind. Such are the *Ars Grammatica*, the *Liber de Definitionibus*, a commentary on the *De Inventione* of Cicero, translations of Porphyry's *Isagoge* and other writers of the Neoplatonic school. On his conversion he abandoned his profane studies without hesitation and gave himself up to the work of expounding and defending the Faith he had embraced.

It was against the Arians that Victorinus directed his keenest shafts. A treatise, *Liber de generatione Divini Verbi*, a tract, *De Homoousio Recipiendo*, and above all, a great work in four books, *Adversus Arium*, testify to his activity in refuting the heretical arguments. We know that he wrote other works on the same subject, but even their titles are lost. Besides refuting the Arians he wrote commentaries on S. Paul, following an original method differing from the traditional interpretations: those on the Epistles to the Galatians, the Ephesians and Philippians still exist and show us his method of exegesis. He also wrote three hymns, *De Trinitate*, and perhaps translated some of Origen's works. In the space of a few years he produced an imposing series of books.

Tradition has been too generous in attributing to Victorinus many writings that are not his. Such are an opusculum, *Liber de Physicis*, by an African of the second half of the fourth century, and two treatises, *Liber ad Justinum Manichæam* and *De verbis scripturæ: Factum est vespere et mane dies unus*, the origin of which is uncertain; as well as some poems: *On the Martyrdom of the Machabees; On Jesus Christ, God and Man;* and *On the Wood (or Tree) of Life.*

S. Jerome is very hard on Victorinus' style, which he finds obscure and unintelligible except to scholars. He believes that the former rhetorician retained, even as a Christian, a preference for the dialectic methods and abstract reasonings that he had learnt in the school of Porphyry. The character of his writings is certainly austere, but he has rendered an immense service to theology by determining its vocabulary and furnishing it with exact terms and strict definitions. He carried on Tertullian's work with a better equipment for its accomplishment in the face of later needs, and this in itself deserves our gratitude.

## IV. *Lucifer*

Whilst the convert Victorinus was writing against the Arians in Rome, a bishop of Sardinia, Lucifer of Cagliari, who had been exiled to the East for the Nicene Faith, was multiplying incendiary pamphlets against those who had driven him from his diocese. The Emperor Constantius had banished him in 355, after the Council of Milan, to which he had been deputed by Pope Liberius, and for five or six years he wandered about in Commagena in Syria, in Palestine and the Thebaid, spreading abroad his violent and angry invectives. The very titles of his works show their bitterness: *That we should not come to terms with Heretics; The Apostate Kings; No one should judge or condemn the Absent; Those who sin against God should not be pardoned; Let us die for the Son of God.* In these books there is

## THE FIRST SIX CENTURIES

neither philosophy nor theology. Lucifer does not think of discussing: he accuses, condemns and strikes. He multiplies quotations from Scripture, particularly the more terrible passages; the invectives of the prophets against wicked kings, and all these he applies to the Emperor Constantius, who is in his eyes the worst criminal of them all. Not from him—Lucifer—are attempts at reconciliation to be sought: in his passion he draws a rigid line which must not be bent.

This becomes evident after the death of Constantius, when the exiled bishop was able to return to his See. Rome was then occupied in dealing with the case of those bishops who had subscribed to the Councils of Rimini and Seleucia, as well as with the many faithful who had fallen into Arianism and whom the Roman See was trying to reconcile. Lucifer would consent to nothing of the sort; to him Arianism was the unforgivable sin, and when, in spite of his efforts, he beheld Pope Liberius pardoning the lapsed he withdrew to Cagliari and formed a small sect entitled Luciferians. He died in obscurity towards 370, unreconciled with the Church for which he had fought so strenuously. His end recalls that of Tertullian, and there is certainly a likeness between the two: the same violence and exaggeration; but Lucifer had not the talent of his predecessor. His style is monotonous, his language uncultivated, and his readers soon tire of his persistent virulence.

Lucifer had some partisans and followers who were more or less talked about between 380 and 390. The best known are the deacon, Hilary of Rome, the author of a lost writing *On the Rebaptism of Heretics*; the priests Faustinus and Marcellinus, who in 383-4 presented a petition to the Emperors Valentinian II, Theodosius and Arcadius in favour of their persecuted brethren; and finally, Bishop Gregory of Elvira. Until the present day this writer's name scarcely occurs in literary history: S. Jerome attributed to him a small book, *On the Faith*, which was thought by some to be the work of Phæbadius of Agen, but fortunate discoveries have lately not only proved the authenticity of the above treatise, but have restored a valuable literary heritage to Gregory: five homilies on the Canticle, twenty on other passages of Scripture, one on *The Ark of Noe*, and, possibly, a treatise *On the different kinds of Leprosy*. Gregory is a severe moralist who takes care not to lead his flock by the way of mercy, but their austerity does not detract from the interest of these sermons, which show us very clearly what was the condition of the Church in Spain from 380 to 390.

Very different from Lucifer and his followers is the former's contemporary, Eusebius of Vercelli, who was exiled and returned to his diocese at the same time as the Bishop of Sardinia. Eusebius also was a firm Catholic and opposed the Arians, but he knew how to show pity and indulgence to the penitent. During his exile he wrote three letters, to Constantius, to his flock and to Gregory of Elvira. After his return he translated into Latin the Psalms of Eusebius of Cæsarea, not without correcting them according to the rules of strict orthodoxy. This translation is lost.

Phæbadius of Agen is also one of the most determined opponents of Arianism in the West. We only possess a small book of his, *Against the Arians*, written in 357 or 358, to condemn the second

## THE FIRST SIX CENTURIES

formula of Sirmium. It is uncertain whether this not very original book was followed by others, and S. Jerome does not seem to have known more of Phæbadius' literary work. In 392 he was living, in extreme old age.

Amongst the models he followed is S. Hilary of Poitiers, who is without doubt the greatest Catholic Latin writer belonging to the heroic period of the Church's struggles with the Arians and the Emperor Constantius.

### V. Saint Hilary

Born in or about 315, S. Hilary belonged to one of the best families of Poitiers. He was brought up as a heathen, but could not there find an answer to the questions that troubled his active mind. Then he read the Holy Scriptures, which were a revelation, and in consequence he embraced Christianity. About the year 350 he was elected Bishop of his native city. At that time Arius and the Council of Nicæa were scarcely known in this remote province of Gaul, and even the Bishop, who read little besides the Bible and the heathen classics, had not heard of the famous Creed of the great Council. A commentary on the Gospel of S. Matthew, which may belong to the years 353 or 355, show the subjects that then interested S. Hilary: he wrote to make his people understand the Gospel History, to explain the literal text and then to show them the spiritual meaning underlying it. Nothing foretold the great struggle that was to be provoked by the interference of Constantius in the affairs of the Church.

The change came in 355, when Gaul learnt the unhappy issue of the Council of Milan, the exile of

THE CHRISTIAN LATIN LITERATURE OF
the defenders of the Faith, Dionysius of Milan, Eusebius of Vercelli and Lucifer of Cagliari. The envoys of the Emperor went about from Church to Church to obtain signatures, and the following year the Council of Béziers registered the defection of the Gallic episcopate. Hilary, however, was roused. Directly he beheld the orthodox Faith in peril he took up his position against the Emperor. After the Council of Béziers he drew up a work crammed with documents and proofs, *Contra Valens et Ursacium*, where he recalls the events of the preceding years and shows up the duplicity of the bishops who acted as counsellors to Constantius.

His courageous attitude brought on him a sentence of exile. Banished to Phrygia he profited by his forced retirement to study the great Doctors of the Greek Church; he read Origen's works; he learnt the details of the Arian controversy and soon felt sufficiently sure of his ground to compose a book, *De Trinitate*, a great dogmatic treatise in twelve books, and one of the most strongly framed productions of Latin theology. Following a definite plan, he gives decisive proofs of the Divinity of the Son and demonstrates the weakness of the Arian argument. Throughout this work S. Hilary shows himself to be a learned exegetist and perfect dialectician, as well as a naturally gifted writer.[1]

Soon after this he heard of the Arian divisions and the attitude of Basil of Ancyra and his group (358); he notes with joy their friendly disposition and hastens to make it known to the Western bishops. Such is the aim of his book *On Synods*, where the documents of the Eastern Councils are placed by

[1] Cf. *The Throne of the Fisherman*, by T. W. Allies, p. 354. (London, Burns & Oates, 1909.)

## THE FIRST SIX CENTURIES

the side of the theological discussions. It is a work of conciliation and peace, full of the hopes that had been raised by the Synod of Ancyra.

Such activity made the Saint known and respected by his Eastern colleagues, who invited him to the Council of Seleucia (359). There he assisted at the ruin of his hopes and the defeat of orthodoxy. Sent to Constantinople to give an account to the Emperor of the Council's sittings, he prepared a detailed report, addressed *To Constantius Augustus*, but an audience was refused him. The Bishop therefore expressed his indignation in a vigorous pamphlet, *Against the Emperor Constantius*, full of such terrible invective that he seems to have felt it would be dangerous to publish it, and it did not appear till after Constantius' death. At the same time he prepared a fresh historical work in continuation of his treatise *Contra Valens et Ursacium*, in order to make the documents of the Councils of Rimini and Seleucia better known, and he drew up a reply—almost entirely lost—*Against the Detractors of the Book on Synods*. His zeal was untiring.

Finally Constantius and his friends became uneasy, and to prevent Hilary's influence from spreading the Emperor was advised to send him back to his distant See. The Bishop therefore returned to Gaul, where he was enthusiastically received. But even there he did not find rest. The Arians were still all-powerful in Milan and Hilary carried the fight into Italy, but without much success. A book, *Contra Auxentium*, the Arian bishop of Milan, relates this incident in the Saint's career and denounces the imposture of his adversary.

It was only after his return from Milan that S. Hilary found peace. His last years were spent in writing exegetical works: a *Commentary on the Psalms*, in which the influence of Origen is evident; the tractatus, *On Job*, almost completely lost; *The Book of Mysteries*, explaining the figurative prophecies of the Old Testament. He also composed some liturgical hymns; three of these are certainly authentic and two or three others may be so. It is possibly during this time that the Bishop put together some documents that he had not used in his previous compilations. We know less of this period of calm than of his years of exile. Even the date of his death is uncertain, but it was probably not later than January the 13th, 368.

S. Jerome, the great critic of Christian literature, is severe in his appreciation of S. Hilary. According to his view the Bishop mounts the stilts of the " high falutin " style (*cothurnus*) of the Gallic writers, and whilst adorning his pages with the flowers of Greek rhetoric, indulges in such lengthy periods as to prevent the simpler brethren from understanding him. It is true that sometimes the Bishop is difficult to follow. His style is strained and artificial; the writer is sometimes too conscious of the means he is employing. But he knows the importance of language and composition in a literary work, and in a humble and touching prayer he begs of God to grant him *verborum significationem et dictorum honorem*. Such a degree of anxiety is rare amongst Christian authors.

But it is unnecessary to exaggerate, as does S. Jerome, the difficulties in S. Hilary's works. Their obscurity more often arises from the complexity of the subjects treated than from the formulas employed. He had to speak of the Trinity with a tongue scarcely accustomed to such a subject. Is it

## THE FIRST SIX CENTURIES

therefore surprising that at the first attempt he should not arrive at perfect clarity?

S. Hilary is in truth a born writer. Assisted by a remarkable classic culture, he knows how to use in the service of theology the highest qualities of a well-informed and assured talent.

## CHAPTER VI

### SAINT AMBROSE AND HIS FRIENDS

I. Saint Ambrose. II. His Contemporaries.

UNTIL the enthronement of S. Ambrose in the episcopal chair of Milan, on December 7th, 374, Italy has scarcely any place in the history of literature. The names of very few writers can be added to Lucifer of Cagliari and Eusebius of Vercelli, who have been already mentioned.

Firmicus Maternus is, however, a very original character, more especially if he is really the author of the astrological work known as *De Nativitatibus sive Matheseos*. If so he would have written it whilst yet a pagan, and after his conversion showed as much ardour in condemning the false gods as he had before done in defending them. But it is not certain that we have to do here with only one writer, and it is sufficient glory for the Firmicus we know, to have written, about 347, the work *De Errore profanorum Religionum*, and, perhaps, in 351, the *Consultationes Zacchaei et Apollonii*, a great controversial work. The first of these books is one of the most curious Apologies that we possess. Not content with bringing the idols to trial and proclaiming the immorality of their mysteries, the author denounces paganism with fury, as the origin of all evil, and implores the emperors whom he

# THE CHRISTIAN LATIN LITERATURE

addresses to extirpate it down to the very roots. His violence and passion, and even the exaggeration of the theses he defends—cleverly enough—make of his book a document that is representative of the whole period.

In another way the famous Liberian *Chronographus* is scarcely less characteristic of the peace finally gained by Christianity. This immense compilation, copied in Rome, in 354, contains, besides a wholly pagan calendar, annals and lists of the consuls and prefects of Rome, a table of Paschal dates between 312 and 411; a list of anniversaries of the Popes from Lucius I to Julius I (*depositio episcoporum*), and of the martyrs honoured in Rome (*depositio martyrum*); a list of the Popes from S. Peter to Liberius (the Liberian Catalogue); two chronicles and a description of the city of Rome. Heathen documents figure by the side of Christian texts. He for whom this compilation was made needed both the one and the other, as did many Christians during the pontificate of Liberius.

The inscriptions composed by S. Damasus for the tombs of the martyrs establish the triumph of the Church, able at last to render a public cult to the victims of the persecutions. Pope Damasus, the successor of Liberius, was a literary as well as a very devout man. In order to honour the martyrs buried in the catacombs he composed epitaphs for the most illustrious of them, which were engraved by the expert calligrapher, Dionysius Furius Philocalus. These inscriptions and some short verses of S. Damasus do not show much poetic talent, for they are mostly as cold as they are correct, but they are valuable for the liturgical information contained in them.

# THE CHRISTIAN LATIN LITERATURE OF

## I. Saint Ambrose

S. Ambrose was not raised to the episcopate till after the death of Pope Damasus. A more unexpected or a more fortunate election has been rarely known than that of the high official, still a catechumen, who, having entered the Church to keep order, left it a bishop, amid the acclamations of the people.

Ambrose was born at Treves, in 333, but was educated in Rome. His noble birth and his own brilliant gifts pointed him out for early promotion, and he had already been made consular governor of Liguria and Æmilia when Providence withdrew him from a civilian position.

Having been elected bishop against his will, Ambrose threw himself wholeheartedly into his new task. He had everything to learn of Christian doctrine, and he read with avidity not only the Bible but also the best Christian writers, particularly those belonging to the East; not content with the ancient authors alone, he kept himself informed of the sermons that were being preached at Constantinople and the latest books from Alexandria. But at the very beginning of his episcopate he had to enter on a struggle with the Arians, who were supported by the Empress Justina. Though Ambrose was a devoted minister of the emperors, who more than once charged him with difficult missions in Gaul, he was not afraid to oppose them even in delicate circumstances. He forbade the re-erection of the altar of Victory in the Hall of the Senate, he refused to give up to Justina a basilica claimed by the Arians, and he imposed a public penance on

## THE FIRST SIX CENTURIES

Theodosius the Great after the massacres of Thessalonica. In the course of an episcopate of twenty-three years (374-397) troubles were not spared him. He rose superior to them all and realized in his own person the model of a perfect bishop and a great statesman.

He possessed all the qualities necessary for this double rôle and his education had wonderfully developed his natural gifts. A supple and alert intelligence enabled him to grasp at once the most difficult questions, whilst his upright and prudent judgment was quick to solve them. His disposition inclined him to moderation and he was an enemy to extremes, whilst his strong convictions saved him from dangerous concessions. His was a thoroughly Roman genius, with a strict sense of justice and an interest in practical matters. Nevertheless he owed to the Greeks the best of his theological knowledge, with something of their subtlety, universal curiosity and love of metaphysical speculation. His whole life shows a happy combination of action and contemplation, and by this perfect union of dissimilar qualities he remains a rare type of humanity.

It is surprising that S. Ambrose should have been able to write in the midst of his multifarious occupations. Most of his literary works are, in fact, sermons and homilies which he afterwards published as treatises. They deal chiefly with moral and practical subjects; his desire is to instruct his people in the Christian life, and he often takes some text of Scripture, explaining it allegorically, after Origen's method, and applying it to some practical end. Often also he is content to expound the chief duties of the faithful, his favourite subject being the praise of virginity. Sometimes, however, circumstances oblige him to treat the grave doctrinal problems raised by the Arian controversy, a duty from which the Bishop does not shrink; but in this case he borrows most of his arguments from the Eastern theologians. His works may therefore be divided into three principal classes: exegetical, dogmatic and ascetico-moral, though this division must not be regarded as arbitrary.

As an exegetist Ambrose comments on the *Hexameron*, in six books, which owe much to S. Basil's homilies on the same subject. He deals also with the Old Testament figures, Cain, Abel, Noe, Abraham and the patriarchs, Jacob, Joseph and others. The Jewish writer, Philo, is here his favourite model, and some passages in these books are in fact translations of the Alexandrian exegetist.

His principal work as a moralist is that on the duties of Christian ecclesiastics, *De officiis ministrorum*, which, in its order and disposition, reminds one of Cicero's book with the same title, which has evidently been used as the Bishop's model. In spite of his efforts to Christianize the precepts of the Stoics on morality and utility, it is easy to perceive in his adaptation, illustrated by Biblical examples, the ancient rules of profane wisdom. But his attempt to give to the Church, and especially to her priests, the moral teaching that was needed is none the less remarkable.

However interesting in its details may be the *De officiis*, the Bishop is evidently far more at his ease in his writings of spiritual direction, where he can expound without restraint his views on asceticism and the perfect life. Four treatises on virginity: *De Virginibus ad Marcellinam; De Virginitate; De*

## THE FIRST SIX CENTURIES

*Institutione Virginis; Exhortatio Virginitatis;* and one, *On Widowhood,* develop with ardour his favourite maxims, and such is the force of conviction in these little books that we can understand the enthusiasm with which they were received by so many Christian maidens in Milan and the whole of Northern Italy.

Most of the Saint's doctrinal writings relate to the Arian controversy: he writes to the Emperor Gratian, *On the Faith* and *On the Holy Ghost;* and a treatise *On the Incarnation of the Lord.* Two books *On Penance* are directed against the Novatians; and a treatise on the Sacraments, *De Mysteriis,* is full of information on the liturgy of the Milanese Church at the end of the fourth century, and testifies to the pastoral zeal of the Bishop.

It is when he treats of theological matters that we see the insufficient preparation of the high civil functionary suddenly thrust into the episcopate, but at the same time we cannot but admire the extraordinary ease of his adaptations and his talent for assimilating other people's ideas. Nearly all his theology is borrowed from the Greeks, from Didymus, S. Gregory Nazianzen, S. Basil, and even in his own day he was reproached for his " thefts." These reproaches were not always very just: S. Ambrose never tried to hide what he owed to others, and even where he borrowed the most he adapted the language of his Greek models to the Latin spirit, making it intelligible and practical for his Western countrymen. By thus preventing the Church of the West from isolating herself and obliging her to gather the best fruits of Eastern thought he rendered her a signal service.

Some occasional discourses show us the official

orator, careful to observe the rules of traditional rhetoric. Whether he preaches the funeral discourse of his brother Satyrus, of the young Valentinian II, or of Theodosius the Great, S. Ambrose is faithful to received custom, and in reading these funeral orations we see that they were written by one who had been formed in the strict methods of the schools. But behind these conventional formulas may sometimes be divined a personal emotion which is sufficient to place the *Consolationes* of S. Ambrose in a higher rank than most of these rather artificial literary productions.

S. Ambrose's correspondence is another witness to his extraordinary activity. We possess ninety-one of his letters, relating to most of the great events in which he took part: the affair of the altar of Victory, the demands of the Empress Justina on behalf of the Arians, the embassies of S. Ambrose in Gaul, the massacres in Thessalonica, the destruction of the synagogue of Callinicum. We should certainly have liked to find these letters a little more intimate and personal, but this was scarcely to be expected of a man occupied as was S. Ambrose. His correspondence is part of the work of his ministry, and though not in the least confidential, discovers to us the secret of a great soul devoted to the fulfilment of its daily duty.

The composition of his hymns also formed part of his ministry. Before him S. Hilary had attempted to give to the Christians of the West a liturgical poetry like to that which formed the charm of the Eastern ceremonial, but his hymns were too learned and complicated to become popular. S. Ambrose was more fortunate; in a simple rhythm that was easy to remember, of iambic dimeter, grouped in strophes of four lines, he sang the splendour of the new-born day, the anxiety of the sinner at the approach of death, the blessed fruits of the Cross, the goodness of God in sending His Son to sinful humanity, the glory of the Apostles and of the Milanese Saints. These hymns, learnt at first by the people of Milan, soon spread throughout the West and very early began to be imitated, so that to-day, among the multitude of " Ambrosian Hymns " that we possess, it is difficult to discover the dozen or so that are really authentic.

As an exegetist, a moralist, a theologian, an orator, letter-writer and poet, S. Ambrose holds a place apart in the history of Christian literature. He is, first and foremost a man of action, an administrator, whilst in the episcopate he displays the eminent qualities of the true statesman. He writes to give orders, to draw up reports, and above all, to continue the work of his oral teaching. We must not expect from him very profound thought nor a strictly individual style. He borrows much from the Greeks, whom he willingly acknowledges as the masters of Christian theology, and he does not waste his time in turning elegant phrases. But he is clear and precise; he says plainly what he sees and desires others to see, and having had a solid classical education he expresses himself in refined and sonorous language. He is always correct, and when he is treating of particularly favourite subjects he reaches the standard of a great writer.

## II. *The Contemporaries of Saint Ambrose*

S. Ambrose's contemporaries naturally grouped themselves round him, and in particular the bishops of Northern Italy, with whom he was in frequent communication. There were many anonymous writers, whose works have come down to us under the Bishop's name. The most celebrated of these is Ambrosiaster (*Pseudo-Ambrosius*), the mysterious author of a valuable commentary on the Epistles of S. Paul and the *Questiones* on the Old and New Testament. It is nearly certain that this writer lived in Rome under the pontificate of S. Damasus, but we can tell nothing more of him. By his side may be placed the author of *De Sacramentis*, probably a bishop of Northern Italy, whose work is valuable for liturgists.

Zeno of Verona is perhaps older than S. Ambrose, but we know nothing of his life, save that he was of African origin and that he left behind a great renown for sanctity. He has left ninety-three sermons on many different subjects, from polemics against pagans, Jews and Arians to powerful exhortations to the more perfect life. These show us a zealous preacher and a pastor, attentive to all the needs of his flock. Written not without elegance, they furnish the historian with much information on the doctrine, the liturgy, the superstitions and the manners of the Christians of Verona about the year 370.

Petronius of Bologna dedicated one of his sermons to S. Zeno on the anniversary of his death; another to an unknown bishop for the day of his consecration. These two discourses are all that this preacher has left us.

We know more of Philastrius, who died Bishop of Brescia before 397, for we possess an important work of his, *On Heresies*, which is more valuable as history than from its rather mediocre style.

# THE FIRST SIX CENTURIES

Philastrius seems to have known the *Syntagma* of S. Hippolytus and used it to describe the ancient heresies, and this gives an interest to his work which the writer's intellectual feebleness would not have gained.

The successor of Philastrius, Gaudentius, dedicated a discourse to his predecessor on the fifteenth anniversary of his death. This sermon, together with about twenty others, published by Gaudentius himself from short-hand notes, reveal a discreet and elegant orator.

Simplicianus of Milan succeeded S. Ambrose, whom he had himself baptized; both the latter and S. Augustine esteemed him highly, and we possess the letters they wrote to him. Gaudentius knew the replies of Simplicianus, but these are now lost.

Vigilins of Trent was also a correspondent of S. Ambrose; there exists a letter of his to Simplicianus and another to S. John Chrysostom, both relating to the martyrdom of Sisinnius and his companions.

Chromatius of Aquileia, to whom is addressed a letter of S. Ambrose, was probably the author of eighteen homilies on the Gospel of S. Matthew, but not of a short explanation of the Lord's Prayer that has been sometimes attributed to him.

We will close this long catalogue with S. Ambrose's deacon, Paulinus of Milan, who, by the desire of S. Augustine, wrote an edifying Life of his Bishop, a little book which satisfies our piety rather than the curiosity of future historians.

Almost all those whom we have named were bishops at the same time as S. Ambrose or very soon after. Their glory is naturally eclipsed by that of the great Bishop of Milan, with whom none

## THE CHRISTIAN LATIN LITERATURE

of them can be compared. But if for a moment we forget him whose contemporaries and, often, friends they were, we must recognize many of them as cultivated men whose works hold an honourable position in a history of literature. They all write correctly and some are not wanting in a natural eloquence that must have roused the enthusiasm of their hearers. At a time when paganism could boast only of Symmachus the best traditions of classical literature had found a home in the Church.

## CHAPTER VII

### SAINT JEROME AND HIS TIME

I. Life of Saint Jerome. II. The Works of Saint Jerome. III. Rufinus. IV. Other Writers.

WHILST Ambrose was making the See of Milan famous, a Dalmatian named Eusebius Hieronymus, after rather an unsettled life, established himself in Bethlehem, where he lived to a great age. S. Jerome was very learned, a great writer and a great saint, but his individuality was so strong and his personality so uncommon that it is almost impossible to judge him impartially. Even to-day he excites either profound sympathy or great antipathy. A book has been written on S. Jerome and his enemies, and one might equally well be composed on S. Jerome and his friends. But in both we should find the same persons, for those are rare to whom Jerome always remained faithful. At our first meeting we discover that we have to do with a passionate soul; when such passion is directed towards a good end, as it was in S. Jerome's case, it can work marvels.

### I. Life of Saint Jerome

S. Jerome was born in or about 347, at Stridon, a small town in Dalmatia, of which the exact whereabouts is uncertain. When he was about twenty he went to Rome to finish his studies under the celebrated grammarian Donatus, and there for a time led a life of dissipation. His reflections, however, together with his visits to the catacombs, in the pilgrimages organized by S. Damasus, and his conversations with friends brought him to see the seriousness of life and he received baptism. A journey into Gaul where he went to Treves awoke in him a desire of the ascetic life, and on his return to Italy he established himself in Aquileia with some friends, amongst whom were Chromatius, Eusebius and Rufinus. For some time they seemed to live in a kind of paradise, and the clerics of Aquileia looked upon themselves as a choir of the blessed.

But this happiness was of short duration. At the end of three years the community was dispersed and Jerome set out for the East. He stayed for a while at Antioch and attended the lectures of the celebrated Apollinaris; then he buried himself in the desert of Chalcis, ever hungering for solitude and perfection, always rebuffed by the indiscretion of the monks, by sickness and also by his perpetual desire for change. He returned to Antioch and was there ordained priest by the bishop, Paulinus, but with the condition of retaining his freedom. Then he went to Constantinople, where he became acquainted with S. Gregory Nazianzen and finally returned to Rome in the autumn of 382.

Jerome had already a reputation for learning and sanctity, and his return to Rome was hailed with delight by both the learned and the devout. The venerable Pope Damasus in particular gave the monk a cordial welcome; he took him as a friend and counsellor and turned his attention to the study

## THE FIRST SIX CENTURIES

of the Scriptures, and it was thought that the Pope wished Jerome to succeed him. But on the death of S. Damasus Siricius was elected to fill the pontifical throne, and then the opposition which Jerome had sustained during the last three years had free play. This opposition arose from his revision of the Gospels, his ascetical propaganda and the influence he had gained over the noble ladies of Rome. Therefore, in the August of 385, Jerome returned to the East.

Then began a long period of stability and calm. In Bethlehem, near the holy places sanctified by the birth of Our Lord, he founded a monastery of men over which he presided: S. Paula organized by its side a convent for women, and the two communities rivalled each other in fervour and holiness. Jerome had discovered his vocation: he devoted himself entirely to the study of Hebrew, the translation and commentary of the Scriptures. He read, he studied, he wrote. But he did not cease to take an interest in all that was happening in the Christian world. Messengers travelled incessantly between Rome and Bethlehem, which became a sort of intellectual centre of the Church. Was there a scriptural difficulty to be resolved? Had some new ideas on virginity, the worship of the saints, or on divine grace, got abroad? Jerome was consulted, and, untiringly, Jerome replied. He multiplied letters, treatises, opuscula. In vain would his tired scribes beg for grace; he would never let them rest. For three or four-and-thirty years he pursued his task.

Trials, however, were not spared him. The saddest of these was his long conflict with Rufinus of Aquileia on Origenism. Rufinus had been the friend of Jerome's youth, the confidant of his riper age. But the translation of Origen's great work *De Principiis* by Rufinus irretrievably separated these two men who were so worthy one of the other, and for many years Jerome, whose heart was torn, felt himself obliged to attack an opponent, who, on his side, kept silence.

Then came the deaths of Paula, Marcella and Eustochium, those valiant women whose piety and affection had supported their father in all his combats. One by one they went to their reward, and Jerome was left alone to bear the weight of years and the burden of contradictions.

Lastly there was the taking of Rome by the Goths; the barbarian invasion of Palestine, the ruin of the monasteries so fondly established, and the mournful arrival of the refugees seeking shelter. All these sorrows found an echo in Jerome's warm and tender heart, and on the 30th September, 419, the venerable hermit died, in the evening of a life wholly consecrated to the service of God and His Church.

In studying S. Jerome's personality the first characteristic that strikes us is his sensitiveness. Few men have possessed a more loving heart than his. His life was a long course of friendships; to those, whether men or women, who gave him their affection he in his turn gave magnificently of his very best. But they must give wholly and without reserve, for that great heart was but too sensible to the pangs of jealousy. He suffered in this way to an extraordinary degree, apparently with no power of resistance. Then he became irascible, suspicious, resentful: he hated as intensely as he loved, and his enemies had cause to fear his passion.

S. Jerome's intellect was not of the highest order;

## THE FIRST SIX CENTURIES

the great metaphysical problems were unknown to him, or if, by chance, he had to handle them, he took only a superficial view. As a true Roman he was chiefly interested in moral questions, and as a moralist he was always inclined to rigorism. Being very impulsive he often wrote without due reflection; some of his writings caused his friends uneasiness, and he had, if not to retract, to explain what he had said, not without embarrassment.

What was wanting to him in breadth he supplied by an untiring application to work. He was a man of great erudition, and had learned almost all that was known in his time, both of profane and sacred science. He read and remembered everything, and the immense number of quotations and reminiscences in his works is surprising. He spoke Greek and Latin, and what is more rare, he knew both Hebrew and Chaldean. He is almost, if not quite, the only one in the Latin Church of the first centuries to consecrate his life to intellectual labours, and in the Greek Church none but Origen can be compared with him. He has left a mass of works, on every kind of subject, and has imprinted on them all the marks of his highly original personality. Like Origen, to whom he owed much, he may be said to have lived on the Bible; the Sacred Books were his daily food, and he translated and commented on them without relaxation. His first work, about 374, was an explanation of the prophet Abdias, and he died before a commentary on Jeremias, begun in 414, was finished. The Church has acknowledged in him the teacher sent by God to explain the Sacred Scriptures and has honoured him with the title of Doctor of the Church.

## II. *The Works of Saint Jerome*

Before he began his great scriptural labours S. Jerome had translated several Greek works; he continued this work of translation for some time, and gave to Latin readers the *Chronicle* of Eusebius of Cæsarea; he completed the portion relating to Roman history, and added a supplement up to the year 378. He also translated the *Onomasticon* of the same author in like manner; the treatise of Didymus, *On the Holy Ghost*; the letter of S. Epiphanius to John of Jerusalem, and several writings of Theophilus of Alexandria, relating to the Origenist controversy; the Rule of Abbot Pachomius and some letters of his and of his successors, Orsiesi and Theodore. Above all, he translated Origen's works: the *Homilies* on Jeremias, Ezechiel, the Canticle of Canticles, the Gospel of S. Luke, Isaias, the *Explanation of Hebrew Names*; and finally, in 398, the four books, *De Principiis*: this last version, almost entirely lost, was valuable from its great fidelity to the original text.

These translations were but as recreations in comparison with his great labours on the Holy Scriptures. Jerome was still in Rome when Pope Damasus asked him to revise the ancient Latin translation of the Gospels by the Greek text. This revision was quickly made; it is uncertain whether it extended to all the books of the New Testament. In any case it excited much criticism from those who wished to remain faithful to the received text. This did not, however, prevent S. Jerome from revising the Psalms of the Septuagint (the Roman Psalter).

## THE FIRST SIX CENTURIES

But soon he was obliged to leave Rome, and from the early days of his sojourn in Bethelehem (386) dates a revision of the Old Testament according to the *Hexapla* of Origen. It was an immense and rather useless work, aiming only at rendering the Latin version more conformable to the Greek, which was itself only a translation. Fatigue, ennui and various accidents, amongst them the theft of his manuscripts, prevented Jerome from finishing this revision, and we only possess the Book of Job and the Psalter (the Gallican Psalter).

Jerome had better work to do than that of revising old translations. He undertook a direct translation of the Old Testament from the Hebrew, and set himself to this task in 391. By 405 the work was finished; it included all the canonical Books, with the exception of some portions of Esther, of Baruch, the Macchabees, Wisdom and Ecclesiasticus. The author could boast that he had erected a monument. It had not been done without contradiction. Scarcely was it begun when objections multiplied. The conservative party refused to believe in the necessity for a new translation: the enemies of the Jews did not approve of being dependent on the Hebrew text; and so on. S. Jerome had to cope with all this opposition, which he did, not without impatience. Naturally, the critics redoubled their efforts when the work was finished, and the author had to continue the fight in defence of his work. He died before the day of victory dawned. But posterity has been just, both to the work and the workman. Under the title of " the Vulgate," S. Jerome's translation has been officially adopted by the Church.

Whilst translating the Scriptures S. Jerome also

commented on them. In order to make known to the Latins Origen's exegesis he translated several of his homilies. His own commentaries owe much to the Greeks and especially to Origen. Perfectly original work must not be looked for; there is scarcely any explanation where we cannot give the name of the model whom Jerome followed. This indefatigable worker had good reasons for making use of the labours of his predecessors; constantly harassed by fresh tasks, pressed by correspondents and stenographers, often suffering from ill-health, he was in many cases obliged to repeat what others had said, and he did this all the more willingly that he had no better exegesis to propose. But we must not think that these many volumes have no personal value. If he imitates, Jerome does not copy: he criticizes, he chooses, he combats. His exceptional knowledge of the Holy Scriptures, his long experience of Palestine and the whole East serve him admirably in his exegetical work. We constantly come across fine symbols and valuable remarks which testify to a very thorough understanding of Scripture. We can still read with profit the *Quæstiones hebraicæ in Genesim*, his commentaries on the prophets, the four Epistles of S. Paul and S. Matthew's Gospel, and even the *Commentarioli* on the Psalms, which has been recently discovered.

Still more interesting are the Prefaces to these commentaries. Nothing can be more vivid and personal than these pages, where Jerome explains how he understands his task, for whom he is working and under what conditions. Here we see the whole man, as we do also in his homilies, one of the most precious discoveries of the last century. S. Jerome is there addressing his monks of Bethlehem, and he talks to them simply, out of his own heart, explaining the Psalms or the Gospel of S. Mark. Those who do not know these discourses are ignorant of one of the most sympathetic aspects in the complex physiognomy of the great scholar. His polemical works show him in quite another character. There is no mildness or piety here, but an implacable force. It was all very well for Jerome to spend his life in demanding peace and seeking it in all sincerity. He loved fighting and was never so much himself as when he had an adversary to overthrow. Opportunities were not wanting throughout his long career, and if they did not present themselves he would provoke them. There were the partisans of Lucifer of Cagliari: Jerome's *Altercatio Luciferiani et Orthodoxi* routed them. Helvidius denied Mary's perpetual virginity: the pamphlet *Adversus Helvidium* reduced him to silence. S. Jerome learnt that the monk Jovinian had attacked asceticism: immediately he leaps up and writes such a decisive Apology for continence that even his friends are alarmed and ask him uneasily if he condemns marriage altogether. When Vigilantius found fault with the veneration of relics and certain other devotions, Jerome dictated in one night a complete refutation of his error. And when the Pelagians began to trouble the Church with their erroneous doctrines on nature and grace the veteran warrior forgot his fatigue and his personal sorrows: in defence of the Faith he found strength to write his three *Dialogi contra Pelagianos*, the extraordinary power of which even his adversaries admired.

But it was against Origenism that Jerome chiefly measured his strength. During some years, from

398 to 402, this controversy absorbed most of his activity. To this end he broke his old friendship with Rufinus and embroiled himself with his Bishop, John of Jerusalem; he opposed S. John Chrysostom and became the translator and panegyrist of the perfidious Theophilus of Alexandria. Nothing availed to stop him, and the silence of Rufinus did not succeed in disarming him. His letter, *Contra Joannem Hierosolymitanum*, and his three books of Apologetics, *Apologetici adversus Rufinum*, are passionate invectives: the arguments are often bad, the reasoning deplorable, but we are carried away by the animation, the biting sarcasm of such books, and it is difficult to study them coolly.

We are glad to find ourselves in a calmer atmosphere on taking up S. Jerome's historical and hagiographical works. The *Lives* of Paul the Hermit, S. Hilarion and Malchus the monk are small masterpieces. They have been the delight of past centuries and might be of our own if we would be content not to expect too great historical precision and to read them in the same spirit in which they were written, as edifying accounts, in which fiction may be lawfully mingled with truth. The treatise *De Viris illustribus* has not the same charm. It is a dull book, consisting of one hundred and thirty-five notices of known and unknown Christian writers, and this merely to prove that the Church had always produced men capable of holding a pen and composing a work. But it is a valuable literary history, in spite of its brevity and too evident traces of the author's rancour.

It has been said with truth that the best of S. Jerome's work is contained in his Correspondence. Such a man could not be a mediocre letter-writer

## THE FIRST SIX CENTURIES

and he raises the art to perfection. His letters deal with many subjects; knowledge, as when he explains obscure passages of Scripture to Pope Damasus, S. Paula, Marcella and others; asceticism, to encourage his correspondents in a love of solitude; piety and devotion; joy and sorrow; anger, hatred and love. Sometimes these letters have a tone of gentle familiarity, whilst others contain passages of real eloquence intended for publication and bear only the exterior form of letters. Such are the obituary accounts of Nepotian, Paula and Marcella; letters of consolation to Paul and Pammachius, and the famous letters to Heliodorus and the same Pammachius, on the perfect life. He has correspondents everywhere, in Gaul and Spain, and even amongst the Goths. The whole world writes to him and he replies to it. We possess about a hundred and twenty-five of his letters, and they give a vivid picture of Christian society at the end of the fourth and beginning of the fifth century. Nowhere do we find so much information on the Church and the faithful than in this admirable collection.

Here, too, we can best appreciate Jerome's supple talent. Neither his translations nor his commentaries show him to us perfectly: the first are too closely bound by the original text and do not reveal the translator's personality, and the commentaries are often hastily composed to impatient stenographers, and made of extracts chosen from all quarters. As to the polemical writings, they often overpass just limits and show us Jerome at his worst. But in his letters we see him as he really is and wishes to be; his frank nature, loyal even when he contradicts himself, and always in good faith. Without effort or affectation, his style attains something like perfection. His knowledge of the Latin of the best period, of Greek and Hebrew, and his long experience in translation enable him to give its full value to every expression.

Posterity has ratified the judgment of S. Jerome's contemporaries, and recognizes him as one of the masters of Latin prose of the Christian period.

### III. *Rufinus*

In our account of S. Jerome we have several times mentioned Rufinus, the friend of his childhood and youth, and the irreconcilable enemy of his later years. It is painful to have to study Rufinus immediately after S. Jerome, for the honest and virtuous translator of many Greek works is but a modest figure beside the great scholar. But life brought them together and history must do the same.

Rufinus was born at Concordia, near Aquileia, about 345, and his friendship with S. Jerome began early. They studied in Rome together, and afterwards both enjoyed in Aquileia those first attempts at monastic life. But in 373 Rufinus departed for the East with the elder Melania, and after rather a long stay in Egypt he went to Jerusalem, where he was to pass the longest and most tranquil years of his life. Strangely enough it was the presence of his friend Jerome in Bethlehem that was to break the course of his austere and peaceful existence. Pitiful jealousies soon manifested themselves between the two Latin monasteries. Then there was a first quarrel, succeeded by a reconciliation. But the

## THE FIRST SIX CENTURIES

translation by Rufinus of Origen's *De Principiis* caused a final rupture. At that time Rufinus had just returned to Italy: interfering friends represented him to Jerome as an intriguer, if not a traitor, and Jerome was wrong enough to believe them. They exchanged more or less cutting letters and wrote more or less passionate *Apologies*. Towards 402 Rufinus gave up the fight. He left Rome for Aquileia and without replying to his adversary's latest book, devoted his last years to works of scholarship. The invasion of Italy by the Goths obliged him to move again, and he fled from the Barbarians to Sicily. He only reached Messina to die, in 410.

Antiquity has rendered homage to Rufinus for his great virtue, his knowledge and his loyalty. Some modern historians have judged him less favourably, being hypnotized by the remembrance of his long rivalry with Jerome, but to-day there is an inclination to judge him more impartially. There is no need to exalt him extravagantly. Rufinus was not a genius and never posed as one. He was simply an intelligent, well-educated man, anxious to do some useful work, and finding in literature the best way of employing his leisure hours. He devoted himself chiefly to translation, and this impersonal kind of work was best suited to his talent.

At the end of the fourth century the Latin-speaking Christians possessed no great theologians and had to depend on those of the Greek school. But there was an increasing number of Latin Christians who, very legitimately, desired to learn the doctrines of the Greek Doctors, whose names, if not their writings, had become familiar to them. Rufinus understood their anxiety and undertook to satisfy it. He therefore translated with untiring industry, devoting most of his labour to Origen: the Commentary on the Canticle of Canticles, on the Epistle to the Romans, some hundred and twenty homilies on the different books of Scripture and, most important of all, the four books, *De Principiis*, were thus placed at the disposal of Latin readers. He also made Latin versions of Pamphilus' *Apology* for Origen, the Dialogue, *De recta in Deum Fide*, the Pseudo-Clementine *Recognitions*, Eusebius of Cæsarea's *Ecclesiastical History*, the *Rules* and eight discourses of S. Basil and nine of S. Gregory Nazianzen; also some short tracts of Evagrius Ponticus, the *Historia Monachorum* of an anonymous writer, and even the curious *Sayings*, or *Ring of Xystus*, according to a Christian revision. Together, these contained the essentials of Greek thought.

The translations of Rufinus are often unfaithful: at that period no one demanded a word-for-word rendering, provided the rules of the art were respected, and great inconvenience was not generally caused by taking some liberties with the original text. Only in the case of the *De Principiis* S. Jerome found fault with Rufinus for having softened Origen's formulas. Rufinus had to justify himself, and his defence is the *Apology*, in two books, full of good and solid arguments, which is certainly the most important of his original works.

Besides the *Apology* there need only be noted another very short *Apology to Pope Anastasius*, two books of *Ecclesiastical History*, which are a poor continuation of Eusebius, a *Commentary* on the Apostles' Creed and one *On the Benedictions of the Patriarchs*. It will be seen that none of these

THE FIRST SIX CENTURIES

carry us very far. In all his writings Rufinus shows himself to be a correct and conscientious author, formed in a good classic school. His style is often rather tame; only in his *Apology* against Jerome does he show any passion, and even there he gives the first place to arguments and facts, being too honest to prefer eloquence to truth.

### *IV. Other Writers*

About the time when Rufinus was translating and continuing Eusebius' Ecclesiastical History, Sulpicius Severus was writing his *Chronicle*. He was a noble of Aquitaine who, after brilliant successes at the Bar and some years of happy marriage, left the world to lead a more perfect life in his villa of Primuliacum. There he spent his time between the practices of asceticism, the duties of friendship and literary composition. The *Chronicorum Libri duo*, or *Historia Sacra*, extends from the Creation of the world to the consulate of Stilicho in 400. It is well and clearly written, and intended to instil a love of history into educated Christians, but it never seems to have found many readers. Much more popular was the *Life of S. Martin*, whose friend and disciple he was. This book, together with three letters, to Eusebius, Aurelia and Bassula on the same subject, and three *Dialogues* on the miracles of S. Martin became during the Middle Ages one of the best known and widely read books of Christian antiquity.

Sulpicius Severus was the friend and correspondent of S. Paulinus of Nola, as was also Nicetas of Remesiana, in the Mediterranean Dacia, now Servia. His is the fine figure of a missionary bishop, at the end of the fourth century, in a remote diocese on the confines of Western Christendom, amongst the Barbarians whom he sought to evangelize. His only relaxation seems to have been two journeys to Italy, where he met S. Paulinus of Nola, with whom he contracted a close friendship and who addressed to him a long farewell poem. Nicetas' days were spent in preaching, and his written works are chiefly catechetical instructions and sermons. Of the most important of these, called, according to Gennadius, *Competentibus ad Baptismum Instructionis Libelli sex*, we possess the whole of the third book on Faith and the Holy Spirit, and the fifth, on the Creed, as well as some fragments of the others. But we have in their entirety two homilies, *De Vigiliis Servorum Dei*, and *De Psalmodiæ bono*, which are full of information on the liturgy; a small treatise to a fallen virgin, *Ad lapsam Virginem Libellus*, and a work of his youth, *On the different Names of Christ*. We learn from S. Paulinus that Nicetas also wrote hymns. Was he the author of the *Te Deum?* Fresh testimony has recently been produced in favour of the hypothesis that to the Bishop of Remesiana, and not to S. Ambrose, we owe this grand Canticle of the Church. It has not yet been proved, but it is a moving thought that this triumphant Chant should have first resounded in the distant regions of Dacia.

Rufinus and S. Jerome were not the first to undertake a pilgrimage to the Holy Land. Some of the many pilgrims of the fourth century wrote accounts of their journey. The oldest is the Pilgrim of Bordeaux, who, in 333, started for Palestine. His journal is little else than an enumeration of the different stages and the distances accomplished. It

## THE FIRST SIX CENTURIES

gives some description of the Holy Land and its curiosities, but retains the dryness of an official guide-book.

Much more vivid is the narration of the Spanish nun, Etheria, or Egeria, who, at the end of the fourth century visited, not only Palestine, but also Egypt, the peninsula of Sinai, Mesopotamia and the tomb of S. Thomas at Edessa. She was a very intelligent and educated woman, who reflected on what she saw and afterwards related it, not without charm. Her narrative, which was intended for her absent companions, was discovered in part in 1887. It is interesting to liturgists for the description of the Holy Week Offices in Jerusalem, and to philologists on account of its linguistic peculiarities, and it is no less interesting to those who would study the mind of an ancient traveller of the female sex.

We must now leave the East and, like Egeria, return to Spain. Here, in the last years of the fourth century, we find a sufficiently rich and animated literature. We have already spoken of Gregory of Elvira. Pacianus, Bishop of Barcelona, was rather younger, and his chief work was that of opposing Novatianism. He wrote much against this old error; amongst others there are three letters *To Sympronianus*, at that time the leader of the sect, *an Exhortation to Penance* and a sermon *On Baptism*. He may also have opposed Manichæism in the treatise *De Similitudine Carnis Peccati*, recently published. Lastly, in the *Cervulus*, one of the most curious of his works, now lost, he attacked certain pagan practices with which some Christians continued to celebrate the New Year. All these writings reveal a very apostolic bishop, anxious for the moral progress of his flock, as well as a writer

## THE CHRISTIAN LATIN LITERATURE OF

of chaste eloquence, as he is described by S. Jerome.

During the lifetime of Pacianus the great Spanish error of Priscillianism was working its first ravages. This heresy is involved in much obscurity; it is not even quite certain in what it consisted. Its leader, Priscillian, began, between 370 and 375, to preach his ascetical doctrines in the region of Emerita. Supported by the bishops Instantius and Silvianus, opposed by other bishops, particularly by Idacius of Emerita and Ithacius of Ossanova, he was condemned by the Council of Saragossa in 380. This condemnation did not prevent him from continuing his proselytism; the bishops who were his friends consecrated him Bishop of Avila, and soon afterwards, being exiled by Gratian, he retired to Aquitaine, where he gained many adherents. But he sought in vain the protection of S. Ambrose and Pope Damasus. Then he appealed to the Emperor Maximus at Treves, and after a long process was finally condemned and executed, together with some of his partisans. The affair made a great noise throughout the West, and in Spain Priscillianism continued to inflame many spirits. It was a long time before calm was restored, and the controversy was not pursued without much expenditure of ink and the composition of many works; it is from this aspect that it interests literature.

Priscillian himself, according to S. Jerome, wrote some opuscula. Are the *Liber Apologeticus* and ten other treatises discovered in a manuscript at Würzburg and published under his name in 1889, really Priscillian's? They were so maintained to be by the first editor, but Dom Morin has since denied this and considers the whole collection as the work of

## THE FIRST SIX CENTURIES

Bishop Instantius, one of the most devoted partisans of the heresiarch. But Dom Morin's hypothesis has not been universally admitted and critics have not spoken the last word on these rather badly-composed works, written in a heavy and ungraceful style, with not very clearly expressed ideas. Priscillian is, however, certainly the author of the *Canons* on the Epistles of S. Paul, a sort of doctrinal résumé of collections from other manuscripts, but which throws no fresh light on his erroneous doctrines. Fragments of some *Letters* are also extant, transmitted by Orosius.

The disciples of Priscillian left some writings, of which we know little more than the titles, with the exception of an anonymous treatise *On the Trinity*, preserved in a manuscript at Laon, and, possibly, an *Epistola Titi de dispositione Sacramenti*, recently published by Dom de Bruyne. Tiberianus and Asarbus (or Asarivus) wrote Apologies, and Dictininus, Bishop of Astorga, composed a book with the strange title of *Libra* (Scales) in defence of lying. The sect also possessed a poet, a certain Latronianus, whom S. Jerome praises for his learning.

Nearly all the Catholic refutations of the heresy have been lost: such as the *Commonitorium* of Hydacius of Emerita, the *Liber Apologeticus* of Itacius of Ossanova, who was perhaps the author of the extant *Contra Varimadum Arianum*; the *De Fide adversus hæreticos*, directed by Audentius against the Manichæans, the Sabellians, the Arians and, more particularly, against the Bonosians; and the *Liber Fidei* by Olympius against the adversaries of free-will. We still possess the *Libellus in modum Symboli*, by the Galician bishop, Pastor,

## THE CHRISTIAN LATIN LITERATURE

which is mentioned by Gennadius, and the *De Fide* of his countryman, Syagrius. Turibius of Astorga lived in the middle of the fifth century and was one of the last opponents of Priscillianism. Besides a letter to the bishops, Idacius and Ceponius, he addressed a *Commonitorium* and a *Libellus* to Pope Leo the Great, which are lost.

Other names might be added to the above, as that of the Spanish monk, Bachiarius, who at the end of the fourth century wrote a treatise *On the Faith*, but whose personality remains very mysterious. The last years of the fourth and the first of the fifth century were for both the Latin and Greek Churches a time of intense intellectual activity. The whole world read and wrote, and took an interest in every kind of problem. S. Jerome was consulted as an oracle on Scriptural difficulties and on the spiritual life by all the regions of the West. In a more complete history than this his correspondents would all find a place. The Greek theologians, both old and new, were studied with ardour, Origen above all, assiduously translated by S. Jerome and Rufinus. The *Pastor* of Hermas was also translated afresh, and Evagrius of Antioch published in Latin S. Athanasius' *Life of S. Antony*. We have reached the period when the cultured classes, after long delays, decided to enter the Church: they brought with them their education, their knowledge and their curiosity, and thus, for a time, even in the midst of the first barbarian invasions, there arose such a blossoming of intellectual life as it is beyond the historian's power to analyse in detail.

## CHAPTER VIII

### CHRISTIAN POETRY IN THE FOURTH CENTURY

I. Various Poets.  II. Saint Paulinus of Nola.  III. Prudentius.

SOMETHING would have been wanting to the admirable expansion of Latin literature in the fourth century if it had possessed no poets. There is no doubt that Christian antiquity was for long insensible to the charm of poetry; its writers were too exclusively apologists and catechists to think of expressing themselves in verse; Commodianus, if, as is supposed, he lived in the third century, was an exception. But after the Peace of Milan the Church had not the same reasons for despising the poets, and the latter began to use their art for the teaching of doctrine. The first Christian poetry was wholly didactic, therefore cold and rather artificial, but obliged, by its very style, to follow traditional rules. Perhaps, indeed, it was as well that these more or less halting attempts should be made before Christian poetry found its wings in the time of S. Paulinus of Nola and Prudentius.

### I. *Various Poets*

After the unknown author of the *Laudes Domini*, a little prayer of 148 hexameters, and the bizarre

Optatianus Porphyrius, who amused his leisure hours by composing poems capable of forming the most unexpected figures or of being read in different ways, the first Christian poet is the Spanish priest Caius Vettius Aquilinus Juvencus, who, about 330, undertook to put the Gospel history into verse. Such an enterprise needed some boldness to begin and some talent to succeed in it. Juvencus had both. His *Evangeliorum Libri*, or Harmony of the Gospels, is cold, long and wearisome, but his verses are correct and harmonious, and show a real poetic talent in the author, as well as a thorough knowledge of classic poetry.

Much more artificial is the Virgilian *Cento* of Proba, a noble Roman lady, who, in the middle of the fourth century, conceived the idea of translating the Biblical narrative into verse, in terms borrowed exclusively from Virgil. It takes much patience and ingenuity to discover her meaning. She wrote 694 hexameter verses, in which, with a little good-will, the reader will find the history of the Creation, the Fall and the Deluge, as well as the Life of Our Lord, from His birth to His ascension.

There is more inspiration in certain little anonymous poems belonging to the end of the fourth century, most of which appear to have been written in Gaul. The themes are various enough and the general style didactic. Thus the *De cruce* celebrates the tree of life, whose marvellous fruits bring salvation to the world; the *De Ave Phœnice*, formerly attributed to Lactantius, chants the glory of the phœnix, re-born from its ashes and the symbol of the resurrection; *De Natura Rerum* is a hymn to the power of God manifested in His works; the *Carmen adversus Marcionem*, which possibly belongs to the

## THE FIRST SIX CENTURIES

end of the fifth century, borrows from Tertullian and others the arguments against Marcionism; *De Sodoma* and *De Jona*, both by the same unknown author, describe, not without skill, the ruin of Sodom and the repentance of Nineveh; the *De mortibus boum*, by Severus Sanctus Endelechius, a friend of S. Paulinus of Nola, is an idyl describing an epidemic among a flock of sheep, who are cured by a miracle, and whose shepherds consequently become Christians.

More practical are the warning *Ad quendam Senatorem* and the *Invective against Nicomachus*. These two pieces, written in Rome at the end of the fourth century, are a curious testimony to the persistence of heathen ideas amongst the aristocratic classes. The first is addressed to a certain great personage, who after having become a Christian had returned to the cult of the *Magna Mater*; the second describes the famous fall of Nimachus and rallies him on the weakness of the gods he adores. They are written with spirit by cultivated men of deep faith.

We find once more Biblical poetry in Cyprian of Gaul, an enigmatic person, even if it is possible to identify him with a priest who from 415 to 418 was in correspondence with S. Jerome. He was the author of a long poem, which is in fact a metrical adaptation of the *Heptateuch*; he may perhaps have prolonged his work, for isolated verses are known on the Books of Kings, Paralipomenon and Job, and certain ancient catalogues mention poetic translations of Esther and Judith. The *Heptateuch* holds an honourable place amongst similar productions. Its author is familiar with the classic poets and shows real skill in the management of rhythm. Some have questioned whether to this writer ought to be attributed the curious and coarse *Cœna Cypriani*, the enigmas of which have not yet been solved, but it is a very unlikely supposition, and the *Cœna* appears to be much later than the date of the Gallic priest.

## II. Saint Paulinus of Nola

Though we remain in Gaul we must go back a few years to speak of Ausonius and his disciple, Paulinus of Nola. Ausonius, the glory of the schools of grammar and rhetoric in Bordeaux, in the fourth century, scarcely figures in Christian literature; indeed, the spirit of most of his works is so manifestly pagan that it has been doubted if he belonged to the Church at all. He was, however, a Christian, though he scarcely shows it. Only a paschal-time prayer, a morning prayer, and a prayer in ropalic verse express his interior sentiments, written in a style of refinement and affectation of rather doubtful taste. The most interesting of his letters in verse are the three last addressed to his favourite disciple Paulinus, when he heard that the latter had renounced the world for a life of asceticism: in these letters there is an expression of real grief at the prospect of the approaching separation, and we here see the best side of the old rhetorician.

Ausonius deceived himself if he thought that his exhortations would keep Paulinus in the world. The disciple replied to his beloved and respected master in two playful letters, written, as though for a last trifling with the art, in verses of different rhythms, but which leave no doubt as to the reality of his

## THE FIRST SIX CENTURIES

conversion. This conversion seems to have been rather unexpected, and even to-day we can hardly penetrate its motive.

Pontius Meropius Anicius Paulinus, born at Bordeaux in 353, belonged to one of the most illustrious families of Rome. By birth and by fortune he was destined for a brilliant career; very early he became a member of the Senate, was a consul in 378 and in the following year was appointed Governor of Campania, where, at Nola, he had large estates. But he soon returned to Bordeaux, where for about ten years he lived the idle life of a great lord. His conversion took place suddenly in 389 or 390. He was baptized by Delphinus, the Bishop of Bordeaux, sold a great part of his lands in Aquitaine and retired with his wife Terasia to Spain, where he lived for some time. He was there ordained priest by the Bishop of Barcelona about the year 394, after which, apparently to avoid the responsibilities of the sacred ministry, he left Spain almost immediately and went back to Campania, to take up the austere life of a monk.

In the town of Nola was the tomb of the celebrated martyr, Felix. Paulinus became the Saint's devout servitor, and the basilica that he built in Felix' honour, which he decorated with frescoes and metrical inscriptions, soon became a place of pilgrimage. The people of the Christian West flocked to Nola, both to honour the martyr and to visit his disciple. Nicetas, the Bishop of Remesiana, went there twice and contracted a close friendship with Paulinus. Thus passed some years of peace and happiness. Then Paulinus had to renounce his tranquillity for good; against his will he was elected Bishop of Nola. It was the period of the Barbarian

## THE CHRISTIAN LATIN LITERATURE OF

invasions and Italy was plunged in misery. Paulinus did his duty admirably. He ceased to write fine poems in honour of S. Felix, and long letters to his friends, and devoted himself to the administration of his diocese. On the 22nd June, 431, he finished his task and went to his reward, leaving behind him a great reputation for sanctity.

All Paulinus' literary works belong to the tranquil years between his conversion and call to the episcopate. This great lord, formed in the best schools of Gaul, was admirably gifted and nothing that he wrote is negligible. Nevertheless he left no great works and never attempted so-called higher studies. His prose legacy consists of about fifty letters and a sermon on almsgiving. But both letters and sermon are finely chiselled and give the impression of being a labour of love; no detail is omitted, no phrase has escaped the file and polish of the master-workman. Even when writing to his friends, and to the best-beloved of them all, Sulpicius Severus, Paulinus would not risk improvisation: it is doubtless his soul that speaks, a tender, faithful and devoted soul; but the scholar is not dead in the ascetic, and he delights, even in his intimate correspondence, to observe the rules of the teachers of rhetoric. Piquant details are not wanting in these letters, so delicately written, full of observation of the world and men, and which contain much information for the historian on Christian life at the beginning of the fifth century.

Paulinus' correspondence was much admired during his lifetime: S. Jerome goes so far as to compare him to Cicero. We still admire it, but his poems are certainly to be preferred. These are the work of a good labourer who will leave no gap in his

## THE FIRST SIX CENTURIES

productions and who handles with consummate art the rarest and most difficult rhythms of classical poetry. But they are still more the work of a true poet whose lively sensibility vibrates to every touch and who finds images of vivid colouring to express his emotions. Paulinus' poems deal, as if at play, with many and various subjects: paraphrases of the Psalms; a panegyric on S. John the Baptist; a sort of Christian *Ars Poetica* dedicated to a certain Jovius; a farewell to Nicetas of Remesiana; a letter of consolation on the death of a child and an epithalamium to Julianus of Eclanum. But by far the most interesting of his poems are the fourteen *Natalicia* in honour of the martyr, S. Felix. From the year of his arrival at Nola till his promotion to the bishopric, S. Paulinus annually composed a poem for the anniversary of his holy patron. The subject-matter may be insignificant, but tenderness and devotion give it life, and there is great variety in these poems, which relate the Saint's miracles, describe his basilica and the crowd of pilgrims who flock to it. In praise of S. Felix Paulinus grows eloquent, and if to-day we find his praises extravagant, we cannot but be touched by their love and fervent piety.

These letters and poems are but the recreations of a highly educated man who, whilst renouncing the world, did not feel bound to renounce the cult of classic beauty, and who in his leisure moments amused himself in writing poetry. Later, as bishop, Paulinus had no leisure moments, and he ceased even to praise S. Felix. But as long as he was master of his own time he praised him with so much delight that we can find no fault. We read with the same pleasure that he had in writing—an effect produced only by the great writers.

# THE CHRISTIAN LATIN LITERATURE OF

*III. Prudentius*

Nevertheless the great Christian poet at the beginning of the fifth century is not Paulinus of Nola, but the Spaniard, Prudentius. Born at Sargossa or in its neighbourhood, in 348, of a noble family, he filled high administrative offices, and was finally appointed to an important post near the Emperor's person. Then he became disgusted with the world and decided to end his days in retirement. At the age of fifty-seven he published a complete edition of his poems, which he had written " to glorify God and atone for the sins of his youth," and to testify to the Faith which henceforth he would serve with his whole soul.

A Preface describes the contents of the book: " May hymns link the days together, and may no night pass without songs to the Lord; may my voice combat heresy, defend the Faith, trample underfoot the sacrifices of the pagans, prepare, O Rome, the fall of idols, utter devout verse to the martyrs and praise the Apostles."

The first of these works is a collection of hymns called *Cathemerinon*, which includes twelve poems to be sung or recited at the different hours of the day and on the great feasts of Christmas and Epiphany. These hymns are very fine and carefully composed, and also very long. Prudentius shows himself to be a master of lyric metre, by the number of rhythms he employs, the richness of his language and the splendour of his imagery. But his poetry is not of a popular kind and only some fragments of the *Cathemerinon* have been preserved for liturgical use;

## THE FIRST SIX CENTURIES

these are the most simple and expressive, and the stanzas in praise of the Holy Innocents, *Salvete flores martyrum*, " are characterized by profound feeling, united to the purest art."

The *Apotheosis* and the *Hamartigenia* are didactic; the first is a refutation of the Patripassians, the Sabellians, the Jews, Ebionites and Manichæans: the second is against Marcionism. These are very grave subjects for a poetic composition, but we can see that in treating them Prudentius makes use of his very varied gifts. He borrows much of his theology from Tertullian and on this builds the subtle and harmonious verses of a poet.

The *Psychomachia* is allegorical, and describes the combats of the virtues and vices, and during the Middle Ages was the most popular of all Paulinus' works. Miniaturists and sculptors have reproduced in Books of Hours and cathedral porticoes the grimacing figures of the vices and the mild countenances of the virtues, and it is from Paulinus' poem that they have borrowed the characteristic features of both. This kind of personification is not to the taste of the present day; the characters are cold and unreal in spite of the poet's efforts to give them life.

Far better is his invective, *Contra Symmachum*, where the Saint's patriotism is happily expressed. He probably only knew the account of Symmachus and S. Ambrose's refutations and was ignorant of the prefect's more recent attacks on Christianity. His Christian faith and Roman loyalty serve him well. None have sung like him the close union of Church and Empire; none have shown such perfect confidence in the eternal destiny of the Roman people. Such confidence seems rather naïve when we remember that it wanted but a few years to the taking of Rome: but it is the confidence of a beautiful soul. Let that suffice.

The *Peristephanon* is in praise of the Apostles and martyrs, especially the Saints of Spain: Emeterius and Chelidonius; eighteen martyrs of Saragossa, the deacon Vincent, Fructuosus of Tarragona, the virgin Eulalia of Emertia, the martyrs of Calahorra; then some Roman martyrs, whose tombs he had venerated during a visit to the capital: SS. Peter and Paul, Lawrence, Cassianus, Hippolytus, Agnes; lastly, martyrs of other countries: Cyprian of Carthage, Romanus of Cæsarea, Quirinus of Siscia. The historian who would seek in these hymns reliable information on the passion of the martyrs would be disappointed. Prudentius accepts every legend, embellishes them with imaginary details and interminable discourses. His hymns, however, bear a unique testimony to the cult of the saints, the veneration of relics and pilgrimages to the Roman catacombs; and in spite of their length, they possess qualities for which they can be read without ennui.

We need not delay on the *Dittochæon*, a collection of forty-nine inscriptions of four verses each, explaining as many scenes from the Old and New Testaments. The title of this collection is obscure and it is possible that the verses may have been intended to explain the mural paintings in some basilica.

What strikes one most in Prudentius' talent is its great versatility. No Christian poet has equalled him in his management of metres and rhythms. His metrical knowledge is prodigious and is not a knowledge of mere theory. He realizes it in practice, and seeking to compare Prudentius with any other writer, Horace's name occurs naturally to the mind.

Prudentius, again, is not merely a clever technicist,

## THE FIRST SIX CENTURIES

he has the poet's soul and temperament. His style is too emphatic, his descriptions too long, his praises turgid: these defects belong, perhaps, more to his country and period than to his personal genius; in any case it would be unjust to dwell too much upon them. Taking him altogether, Prudentius, as a poet, stands in the first rank.

There is something very remarkable in this blossoming of Christian poetry at the end of the fourth century, and it is scarcely explained by the peace in the Church and the conversion of the educated classes. The same causes were acting in the East, but produced no real poets among the Greeks, for Gregory Nazianzen, the only one who attempted to write in verse, was little more than an amateur. On the eve of the taking of Rome there was an ephemeral renaissance in the West: men like Symmachus, Claudianus, Rutilius Namatianus hold an honourable place in the history of literature, but inspiration is wanting and their balanced cadences and lengthy periods are of the school. Only in Christianity does that Faith raise up writers. Paulinus of Nola and Prudentius are not only the foremost of their time; they shed a light of glory on all Latin poetry.

# CHAPTER IX

### SAINT AUGUSTINE

I. Life of Saint Augustine. II. His Works.

S. AUGUSTINE dominates all the Christian literature of his period as he dominates the whole history of the Church during the first thirty years of the fifth century. One is lost in admiration at the number of his books, yet they represent but a part of his extraordinary activity. S. Augustine was first and foremost a priest and bishop; he wrote in fulfilment of the duties of his office and to extend the work of his apostolate.

## I. Life of Saint Augustine

He was born at Tagaste, a small town in Numidia, on the 13th November, 354. His father, Patricius, was a pagan, but his mother, S. Monica, was a devout Christian, and Augustine's childhood was profoundly influenced by this holy woman, who united a fervent piety to great good sense and patience. Augustine studied with great success, first at Tagaste and then at Madaura, after which he went to Carthage to perfect himself in rhetoric, law and philosophy, and in every other science, for his passion for knowledge was insatiable. This, how-

## THE CHRISTIAN LATIN LITERATURE

ever, was not the only passion that governed his ardent nature; he became a slave to earthly love, and in 372, when he was only eighteen, he formed an illicit union with the woman who became the mother of his son, Adeodatus, and with whom he remained entangled throughout his years of study.

When he was quite a child his mother had his name entered as a catechumen, but she did not have him baptized. And Christianity attracted neither his mind nor his heart. Cicero's dialogue, *Hortensius*, which he read towards 373, might have drawn him to the Church, for it enkindled in him an intense desire to possess truth in its integrity. But, after going rapidly through the Holy Scriptures, he was disgusted at their style and their allegories, and turning from the Catholic Faith, he allowed himself to be seduced by the promises held out by the Manichæans. He belonged to their sect for nine years, and even made some proselytes. But he was restless: exteriorly he pursued successfully the career of teaching he had adopted: after having taught grammar at Tagaste, then rhetoric at Carthage and Rome, he received an official professorship at Milan. It was at this time also that he wrote his first books: a poem which gained him the prize in a "poetic tournament," when the celebrated Vindicianus conferred upon him the *corona agonistica*; a treatise on *Beauty and Order*, dedicated to the advocate Hierius, and a panegyric on the consul Bauto, preached at Milan, the 1st January, 385.

All this was, however, but the exterior of his life. He was still seeking for that Truth, on the conquest of which *Hortensius* had determined him. His mind became gradually detached from

Manichæism, as its weakness became clear. For a short time he turned to the teaching of the New Academy, with its pessimistic scepticism, but found there nothing but a passing intellectual amusement. The books of the Neoplatonists, which he read in 385, finally revealed to him the existence of a spiritual world and helped him to the solution of the problem of evil.

But before receiving baptism Augustine wished to test the Faith he had discovered. Like Newman at Littlemore, he retired to Cassisiacum, in the neighbourhood of Milan, with some friends, and there, for several months he thought and prayed. His philosophic dialogues date from this time of repose. But the dolorous crisis had passed and the happy inhabitants of Cassisiacum found that the questions they then discussed among themselves, however interesting, no longer roused them to passion. Peace reigned in their souls, and it is this peace that we find in these books, where an occasional cry of thanksgiving to God is all that recalls past troubles.

On the 24th of April, 387, Augustine received baptism from the hands of S. Ambrose in the basilica of Milan. With him were baptized his friend Alypius and his son Adeodatus. There was nothing now to keep the neophyte in Europe, and he immediately started for Africa, accompanied by his mother and all those who having shared the anguish of his doubts, now desired to pursue with him a life of Christian perfection. But Monica was not to return to her native country. She died of fever at Ostia, only a few days after a conversation with her son of such marvellous beauty that she seemed to have touched the infinite. This unexpected death and several other complications delayed their departure,

## THE FIRST SIX CENTURIES

so that the travellers had to spend the winter of 387, and the first months of 388 in Rome.

At last, in the autumn of that year Augustine was able to settle in Tagaste. The little town where he had passed his childhood was to be the scene of his new life as an ascetic. He and his friends formed themselves into a sort of monastery and for three years lived together in peace, their happiness only troubled by the death of the young Adeodatus. Having given his mother up to God, Augustine had now to give Him his son, and thus were finally broken the chains which might have bound him to the past and so have prevented him from devoting himself wholly to the service of God and souls.

Henceforth this service was to absorb and devour him. Up to now Augustine had belonged to himself: now, perhaps without knowing it, he was ready to become the man and the property of others. One day, towards the end of 391, he went to Hippo, where the people claimed him and insisted on his becoming a priest. In vain he resisted, declaring his weakness and unworthiness; the following spring Bishop Valerius ordained him, charging him with the ministry of preaching, and three years later chose him as his coadjutor. In 396 the Bishop died and Augustine was elected as his successor. His history then became the history of the Church of Africa.

It would be impossible to trace this history, even in its broad lines, and in recalling the salient facts we should still miss the essential, namely the spirit of S. Augustine which animates and enlightens it. He had to face difficulties of every kind. Scarcely had he finished refuting the Manichæans and Donatists than he had to combat a new heresy that was all the more dangerous for being more insidious, that of the British Pelagius, and this heresy Augustine had to oppose up to his death. He took part in councils, he organized public discussions, he replied to discourses, he multiplied books; he neglected no means to assure the triumph of Catholic Truth. His influence spread beyond Africa; it extended widely in Gaul, Italy and Spain; everywhere he had correspondents who questioned him and to whom he replied, and there were none, even to S. Jerome, who did not co-operate with him in their efforts to crush Pelagianism. But besides these great problems Augustine had to deal with many humbler questions of daily life: homilies to be preached in his basilica, reports of his diocesans to consider, the goods of the Church to administer, quarrels between Catholics and Donatists to be appeased, the recruitment of his clergy, the instruction of the native peasantry who knew no Latin and spoke only Punic. Augustine thought of everything and neglected no detail.

He spent thirty-five years in this active and devoted life. His last days were saddened by the Barbarian invasions that laid Africa waste. The Vandals were approaching Hippo and soon laid siege to the city. Alone, Augustine upheld his people's courage and raised their hopes. Then he died, on the 28th of August, 430, and was thus saved the sight of the taking and pillage of the city he had so greatly loved.

There was nothing small or insignificant in this noble life, wherein are to be found none of the weaknesses that disfigure so many great minds. One is perhaps chiefly struck by the gift of universal sympathy which he possessed in such an eminent degree. His mind was broad enough to understand everything and his heart was large enough to embrace all. It is true that he desired only the triumph of Truth, but even in the most subtle errors he took pleasure in disentangling the portions of truth they might contain, in order to find a solid ground on which to meet his adversaries. Should we, in fact, use the word "adversary"? To Augustine all men were brethren and his polemical treatises are admirable monuments of peace and concord. The long trials that he had himself gone through before attaining to the Truth made him diffident of his own judgment and compassionate to the errors of others; above all they filled him with a deep sense of human weakness and the power of God, by which alone man is raised, above himself and the sin in which he is born, to the possession of divine grace. This sense dominates Augustine's whole work; it penetrates him—not without fear at the thought of the divine judgments—with a tender piety, an ever-grateful love for Him Who had drawn from the mire of sin His servitor and the son of his servant: thus in him are combined an ardent mysticism and a wonderful intellectual power, and these, taken together, raise him above the ordinary types of humanity.

## II. Saint Augustine's Works

This great man, one of the purest geniuses of the human race, was also a very great writer. He did not seek to be such. In his sermons he easily drops into the familiar language of his hearers, occasionally introducing a play upon words or a pleasantry when he thinks this will help the people to understand him better. But by nature he rises higher. He has studied the best authors. With Virgil and Cicero he is so familiar that his language approaches theirs. He possesses also the gift of expressing clearly what he thinks and feels—a gift that is not so common as some pretend. He is never one of those who write, having nothing to say, or who hide the simplest ideas under obscure phrases. When he speaks of what he has at heart—and what has he not?—he is singularly impressive. More than any writer Augustine " has caused salutary tears to flow." Purists may perhaps reproach him with being too much " of his time," and may amuse themselves with picking to pieces his defects—for we are far from pretending that he has none. But let them criticize: we are content to admire. When all is said, Augustine remains the perfect model of the Christian writer and thinker.

Amongst his books, two hold the first place: the *Retractations* and the *Confessions*, for they influence the whole world. The *Retractations*, dictated in 427 or 428, are one of his last works. Having nearly reached the term of his earthly career, the great Bishop reviews all that he has published since the far-off days of his youth, the ninety-three works of his pen. He examines, revises and judges them; one by one they pass before his tribunal, and any formulas or doctrines that he now finds reprehensible are carefully corrected. We know few literary examinations of conscience as sincere and moving as this.

The *Confessions*, composed in or about 400, take us back to the first days of S. Augustine's episcopate. In the mind of the author they are a hymn of praise and thanksgiving to the glory of God, Who has led

## THE FIRST SIX CENTURIES

him by the hand from the darkness of error to the mansion of light. Augustine there relates his childhood, his stormy and passionate youth, his intellectual crises and his long seekings. He closes his story with his preparations to return to Africa, and in the last books he sings without restraint of the benefits of God that shine in all creation. Few books have been more read and meditated than these *Confessions*. Nothing, in the whole of literature, can be compared to this canticle where the humility of the avowal is so intimately united to the splendour of divine love.

Between the *Confessions* and *Retractations*, or, to be more exact, between the conversion and the death of S. Augustine, come the long series of his letters. We possess more than two hundred, and can only regret those that are lost. His correspondence does not perhaps offer as great a variety and interest as does that of S. Jerome; many portions of it are real treatises, and even in the others Augustine rarely mentions himself. Nevertheless, we there find and hear him, together with those who were his friends and confidants; and these letters are also precious as showing us the society by which the Bishop was surrounded.

It would be difficult to give any exact idea of S. Augustine's literary activity, were it not that most of his writings range themselves naturally in a logical and chronological order, which enables us to classify them. The different problems that he had to solve presented themselves successively before him, so that we can, as it were, watch their progress and development.

The first are works of philosophy and rhetoric; they occupied Augustine before his conversion and particularly during his stay at Cassisiacum, when he was seeking to establish a rational foundation for his faith. This was more or less the object of the books, *Contra Academicos, De Beata Vita, De Immortalitate Animæ, De Ordine,* and two books of *Soliloquies.* After his baptism he wrote *De Quantitate Animæ,* and a little later, *De Magistro,* which is in a way his farewell to philosophy. Long before his conversion, and until after his return to Africa, he had written treatises on the liberal arts, which were to have formed a great encyclopedia analogous to that of Varro, but the work was never finished. He wrote *On Grammar* and *On Music,* and drew up the principles of dialectics and rhetoric, but went no further. Other and more urgent subjects claimed his attention.

On his return to Africa Augustine was at once called to combat Manichæism; he had belonged to the sect, he knew their writings; he knew also the ravages they were working among his countrymen, and he felt it to be his absolute duty to attack these lying teachers and unmask them publicly. One after another he struck his blows: *De Moribus Ecclesiæ Catholicæ et de Moribus Manichæorum, De Libero Arbitrio, On Genesis against the Manichæans, On the true Religion, On the two Souls against the Manichæans, On the Nature of Good.* He pitilessly refutes the works on which the sectaries supported their theories, the *Disputationes* of Adimantus and the *Epistle of the Foundation of Mani,* the great book by the learned and pretentious Faustus of Mileve, and the *Letter of Secundinus.* Augustine did not fear public discussions with his opponents, and the stenographed notes of these are extant: in 392 Fortunatus and in 404 Felix held disputations

## THE FIRST SIX CENTURIES

with him. The campaign was pursued with vigour and was prolonged from 388 to 405. In 415 Augustine took it up again momentarily in a short treatise to Orosius *Against the Priscillianists and Origenists*.

But the Donatists were more dangerous than the Manichæans. Before his ordination Augustine had had little to do with them, but as priest and bishop he constantly came across them and realized their danger to the Church. Under his initiative or with his encouragement the African Councils took increasingly rigorous measures: the Bishop convoked conferences and multiplied refutations; he ceased not till he had gained the victory. In order to stop their propaganda, he composed, in 393, the *Psalmus contra partem Donati*, a rhythmic song for popular use; then he assaulted the schismatics' position and published *Contra Epistolam Donati, Contra Partem Donati, De Baptismo contra Donatistas, De Unitate Ecclesiæ*, and many other tracts that have been lost. He left no Donatist book unanswered: he wrote *Contra Epistolam Parmeniani, Contra Cresconium, Contra Petilianum*, who had written a work *On the One Baptism*. After the decisive conference of 411, Augustine published a Summary of its Acts and an *Address to the Donatists after the Conference*, as well as a letter to Emeritus, the Donatist Bishop of Cæsarea. He preached at Cæsarea in the presence of Emeritus and held a public disputation with him, which was taken down by the stenographer. Finally, towards 420, he replied to the letters of Gaudentius of Thamugadi. Then the campaign closed. The Donatists were vanquished and ceased to be a danger to the Church of Africa.

After this there arose a new heresy, against which

Augustine had to oppose his whole strength. Pelagianism denies the necessity of divine grace and imperils the very foundations of the Faith, and the Bishop had need of all his indefatigable zeal to crush his tenacious and subtle adversaries. From 412 his books succeeded one another without interruption: *De Peccatorum Meritis et Remissione, De Spiritu et Littera, De Natura et Gratia, De Gestiis Pelagii, De Gratia Christi et de peccato originali, De Nuptiis et concupiscentia, De Prædestinatione Sanctorum, De Dono Perseverantiæ, Contra Julianum, De Correptione et Gratia.* A tract Against the Second Reply of Julian is unfinished. The pen fell from the valiant worker's hand before he could complete his work. But the titles we have given, and many of these designate very important works, suffice to show the immensity of his task. It is true that in this " good fight " Augustine had auxiliaries; but he was the head and it was he who always gave the signal for attack.

The Arians also occupied Augustine. It is true that they had never attained great success in Africa, in spite of their attempts to ally themselves with the Donatists; but their heresy was still sufficiently alive to need refuting. Against them Augustine wrote his fifteen books *De Trinitate*, an immense work which occupied him for seventeen years, from 399 to 416. Here he is not content with refuting heretical doctrines, but takes even greater pains to develop and prove the Catholic theses, and if he does not always avoid obscurity, he presents the general traditional teaching with a rare happiness of expression. It is easy to understand the influence exercised by this book during the following centuries. The treatise *Contra Sermonum Arianorum*, and the

## THE FIRST SIX CENTURIES

*Collatio cum Maximino Arianorum Episcopo* were written for special occasions, and reveal the watchful sentinel always ready to see danger and give the alarm to his people. A small book, *Against the Jews*, and another against heresies in general complete Augustine's polemical works.

A bishop has not only to fight against error; he has also to instruct his people; the explanation of Scripture, the expounding of dogma, instruction on the rules of morality, all these form an integral part of his duty. Throughout his episcopate S. Augustine wrote books of exegesis, of dogmatic and moral theology, and in enumerating them it will be necessary to follow the order of their different subjects.

As an exegetist he commented on the first chapters of Genesis, not only in the *De Genesi contra Manichæos*, but also in *De Genesi ad litteram imperfectus liber* and *De Genesi ad litteram*, but in these he did not get beyond the first three chapters. The seven books of *Locutiones in Heptateuchum* and another seven of *Quæstiones in Heptateuchum* explain detached passages of the Heptateuch, as do the *Adnotationes* on Job. The *Enarrationes in Psalmos* are partly homilies, but in part also they are dictated commentaries. The four books *De consensu Evangelistarum* are devoted to the solution of the important problem of the divergences between the Gospel narratives. Two books on *Evangelical Questions*, two on the *Sermon on the Mount*, an Explanation and Commentary (unfinished) on the Epistle to the Romans and a Commentary on the Epistle to the Galatians, 124 *Homilies* on the Gospel of S. John and 10 on his first Epistle, show the zeal of S. Augustine in explaining the Sacred Books. He has given us a valuable explanation of his method in the *Doctrina Christiana*, which is a veritable treatise on hermeneutics and at the same time teaches what should be the intellectual formation of the Christian doctor.

To dogmatic theology belong, among others, the *Enchiridion*, a summary of Christian doctrine addressed to Laurentius; a sermon *On Faith and the Symbol*, the treatise *On Faith and Works*; the books, *On Illegal Marriage*, *On Prayer for the Dead*, and three important collections of Questions on various subjects.

As a moralist Augustine treats the great questions of the Christian's daily life: such are *The Christian Combat*, *The Mirror*, two works *On Lying*; books on Continence, Patience, Fasting, Wedded Life, Virginity, Holy Widowhood, the Labour of Monks, etc. The Bishop interests himself in them all, and to each class of the faithful he gives appropriate counsel. His teaching is certainly austere, but neither harsh nor strained: it aims at forming solid and joyous Christians, full of confidence in the Divine Goodness. After his own many experiences of life he has earned the right to advise others, and nothing is more admirable than the moderation of his words. An absolute theocratist when upholding the rights of God in the gifts of divine grace, Augustine speaks in gentle and paternal accents when instructing his flock on their duty and eternal destiny. The book *De Catechizandis rudibus* deserves special mention: it is a little manual in which the Bishop instructs a deacon of Carthage how to teach Christian doctrine; it is of great value and was largely used in succeeding centuries.

We need hardly remind ourselves that Augustine

## THE FIRST SIX CENTURIES

preached even more than he wrote. And it is in his sermons that we know him as he really was to the Christians of Hippo and Carthage. Most of his homilies were taken down by stenographers as he spoke, and were never revised for publication. Some he made into treatises, and it is easy to measure the distance that separates these latter from those that have been left in their original condition. Happily, we possess a great number of Augustine's sermons: Christian antiquity read, copied and imitated them, so that apocryphal texts are often to be found in the manuscripts side by side with the authentic ones, and the apocrypha themselves contain much that is S. Augustine's. Criticism of the sermons, begun with admirable erudition by the Benedictine Fathers of S. Maur, goes on even to the present day, and the methodical search of libraries is constantly revealing both isolated discourses and complete collections of authentic sermons, so that it is impossible to fix the exact number of Augustine's homilies.

These homilies present the most living picture possible of Christian Africa at the beginning of the fifth century. The Donatists, the Manichæans, the Pelagians, then the Barbarians, cross the stage: the great patrons of the African Church, especially S. Cyprian, are invoked in their basilicas; we follow the instructions of the catechumens and their baptism; the consecration of a bishop, the dedication of a church, the great feasts of Our Lord and the Saints, the many events of daily life, all are described by the Bishop in language that is at times familiar, but often rises to solemnity. By its richness and variety Augustine's eloquence is beyond comparison with any other.

# THE CHRISTIAN LATIN LITERATURE OF

We have intentionally left to the last the Saint's greatest work, *De Civitate Dei*, The City of God, which was begun in 413, but only finished thirteen years later, in 426. The first occasion of the work was the taking of Rome by Alaric and the Goths, and it was intended to be a reply to the pagans who attributed the catastrophe to the abandonment of the ancient worship. But gradually Augustine's horizon widens and " in a burst of genius he creates the true philosophy of history." The fall of empires, the ruin of civilizations, even the taking of Rome, are but passing events. What matters to the believer the disappearance of the most beloved of earthly cities, whilst the City of God, where alone reign peace and beatitude, lasts eternally? Thus our thoughts are raised above human events and passing phenomena to find our true rest in God.

The Middle Ages lived on these ideas, which our greatest Popes have essayed to realize here below, as far as earthly conditions allow; and on them we still live, though scarcely hoping to find the heavenly City in this world, but awaiting with confidence the moment when its gates will be opened to admit us in our turn. Thus the City of God has been, and still is, one of the great books in which men cease not to seek the lessons of life.

It has been written of S. Augustine that " from distant Africa he enlightens all Christianity. To the men of his own time he spoke useful words. He explained to them their own souls, he consoled them in the sorrows of this world, he guided their minds through its mysteries. He was good to all. Through him fanatics were appeased, the ignorant enlightened, the thoughtful maintained in their traditions. He taught the Middle Ages. Even

## THE FIRST SIX CENTURIES

now, after the inevitable decay of long years, he remains the great theological authority. It is by him that we are in communion with Christian antiquity. In many ways he may be said to belong to all times. His soul—and what a soul!—has passed into his writings, and there it yet lives."

## CHAPTER X

### FRIENDS AND ENEMIES OF SAINT AUGUSTINE

I. Saint Augustine's Adversaries. II. His Friends.

For a time the whole thought and letters of Western Christianity seemed to revolve round S. Augustine as from a centre of activity. His enemies were the heretics whom he so persistently refuted; his friends and disciples were nearly all the Catholics in the first half of the fifth century, who felt his influence and lived by his teaching, not, however, without sometimes giving it so striking a form as would have wounded the Master Himself.

### *I. Saint Augustine's Adversaries*

The *Letter* of Mani and the *Disputations* of Adimantus do not concern us here. But Faustus of Mileve was, at the end of the fourth century, the great celebrity of Manichæism in Rome and Carthage, and it was after having discovered this leader's powerlessness to satisfy his search for knowledge that Augustine began to detach himself from the sect. Faustus wrote a long work which Augustine attacked as soon as he became Bishop, and of which we thus know a large portion.

# THE CHRISTIAN LATIN LITERATURE

Secundinus was a contemporary of Faustus, but all we know of his is a letter addressed to Augustine and refuted by him. These are the only two names to be cited, which seems to prove that Manichæism, about the year 400, was not supported by great intellects.

We have already named Augustine's Donatist adversaries. The Pelagians remain to be noticed, and some of them are of a high order. The founder of the heresy, the British Pelagius, appears in history in or near 400, when he was living as a devout monk in Rome. After the taking of the city by Alaric, he went to Africa and thence to Palestine, where his doctrine was accepted by the two councils of Jerusalem and Diospolis. Excommunicated in 417 by Pope Innocent I, then, in 418, by Pope Zosimus, who had at first absolved him, he disappears, and we know his end as little as we know his origin.

Pelagius was an educated man and wrote much. A work which seems to have been orthodox, *De Fide Trinitatis*, in three books, is lost. A long letter to Demetrias, a profession of faith addressed to Pope Innocent I, in 417, some fragments of works *On Nature* and *On Free-Will*, together with some letters, acquaint us with his doctrine and the evasions with which he sought to deceive his judges. Lastly an important *Commentary* on S. Paul's Epistles enables us to judge of his exegesis. This Commentary has raised much controversy amongst the critics which does not so far appear to be ended.

The most active of Pelagius' disciples was Celestius, probably an Italian, who after living with Pelagius in Rome for some years, accompanied him to Carthage, where he was condemned in 411; he then went to Ephesus and Constantinople, returned to Rome, and finally went back to Constantinople, where he died in 419. He expounded his leader's doctrine in numerous *Libelli* and *Opuscula*, from which S. Augustine copied the important passages which he refuted. One of these *Libelli* was addressed to Pope Zosimus. Some letters and a treatise, *Definitiones*, are known to us by their titles or from extracts.

Julian of Eclanum holds a place of his own in the history of Pelagianism, for he seems to have been the most remarkable of its theorists. He was related to S. Paulinus of Nola, who wrote his epithalamium, and was for long a friend of S. Augustine. But this did not prevent his siding with Pelagius and becoming his ardent defender. He dedicated his learning and talent to the cause of heresy, and Augustine had no more redoubtable adversary. Julian opened hostilities by publishing, in 419, four books, *Ad Turbantium*, then, in 421 or 422, eight books, *Ad Florum*: S. Augustine's refutations have preserved a good many fragments of these important works. Julian seems not to have been content with writing only theological treatises; a Commentary on Osee, Joel and Amos has recently been attributed to him, as also one on Job, and another on the Psalter, which last, however, seems doubtful.

The deacon Anianus of Celeda is chiefly known by a Latin translation of some of S. John Chrysostom's homilies: he thought to find in them arguments in favour of Pelagianism, and thus to furnish the heresy with a new weapon. But Augustine intervened on more than one occasion to withhold the great bishop's support from the heretics.

## THE FIRST SIX CENTURIES

Lastly, the British bishop, Fastidius, appears to have written a treatise *On the Christian Life*, addressed to a certain Fatalis and preserved without its author's name, and also a book *On Widowhood* which forms part of the pseudo-Augustinian Apocrypha. This writer is scarcely known to us except by a notice of Gennadius; recent labours have brought him to light.

No doubt the apocryphal and anonymous literature contains some Pelagian writings, such for instance as *The Hardening of Pharaoh's Heart*, discovered by Dom Morin, but we cannot attempt here to search through this literature.

### II. Saint Augustine's Friends

Far more interesting are Augustine's friends, and the majority of African bishops in the beginning of the fifth century deserve the title. The first place belongs to Aurelius, the Bishop of Carthage, an admirable man, who understood S. Augustine and was always faithful to him. Some short discourses and a letter to the bishops of Byzacene are all the literature he has left us. Erodius of Uzalis may have been the author of a treatise *On Faith, against the Manichæans*, preserved amongst the works of S. Augustine. Four letters to the Saint and one to Valentinus of Hadrumetum complete our knowledge of him, and the two books, *On the Miracles of S. Stephen*, written at Uzalis, in 420, show us the religious condition of his diocese. Possidius of Calama has left a Life of S. Augustine and a list of his writings, both precious documents and the works of a particularly well-informed witness. We possess two letters on the Nestorian controversy by Capreolus, who succeeded Aurelius in the See of Carthage, but of S. Augustine's other correspondents, Alypius of Tagaste, Fortunatianus of Sicca, Fortunatus of Constantine, Novatus of Sitifis, we only have some allocations pronounced at the conference of 411.

Quodvultdeus, to whom S. Augustine dedicated his treatise *On Heresies*, and who became, in 437, Bishop of Carthage, held no place until recently in literary history, but Dom Morin has drawn the attention of critics to him by claiming him as the author of twelve homilies preserved under S. Augustine's name. It is thought likely that he is also the author of a *Liber promissionum et prædicationum Dei* which is placed among the works of Prosper of Aquitaine. This Bishop, who was driven from Africa by the Vandals and died in exile, thus acquires new importance and shows himself to have been a generous and faithful soul.

The African, Marius Mercator, was acquainted with Augustine from 418, and addressed to him two short tracts, now lost, against Pelagianism. We lose sight of him till 429, when he was at Constantinople, where he fought Pelagianism and wrote to Julian of Eclanum. A *Commonitorium super nomine Cælestii*, written in Greek and translated into Latin by the author, and a *Commonitorium adversum hæresim Pelagii et Cælestii, vel etiam scripta Juliani* date from this period and show that Marius Mercator remained faithful to the defence of orthodoxy. Mercator also occupied himself with the beginnings of the Nestorian controversy: he wrote a short comparison between the teaching of Nestorius and that of Paul of Samosata, translated some sermons

## THE FIRST SIX CENTURIES

and letters of Nestorius and also some portions from Theodore of Mopsuestia. Mercator was a man of documents and dossiers, and neither his original work nor his translations show much style; they are dry and colourless, clearness being their chief virtue.

Amongst S. Augustine's intimate friends was the Spanish priest, Paul Orosius of Bracara in Galicia. The fame of the Bishop of Hippo drew him from his native country to Africa in 414. He prepared for Augustine a short *Commonitorium* against the errors of the Priscillianists and Origenists, begging him to refute more thoroughly the impious doctrines there denounced. Augustine received his request with favour and kept the young priest beside him. However, during the spring of 415 Orosius set sail for Palestine, charged by S. Augustine with a letter to S. Jerome on the origin of the soul. He found a fierce battle going on in Bethlehem; Pelagius was trying to spread his doctrines in Palestine and Jerome was struggling firmly against the heresy. Orosius was a useful recruit and was immediately enrolled. At the end of 415 he published a *Liber Apologeticus*, but the council of Diospolis welcomed Pelagius and his followers. Weary of the fight, Orosius returned to the West and rejoined Augustine. There, at the suggestion of the Bishop, he composed his great work: *Historiarum adversus paganos libri Septem*. These Histories are a sort of supplement to Augustine's *City of God* and have an apologetic aim. They recall all the great events of history, from the creation of the world up to the year 417, and prove that Christians are not responsible for the sufferings of humanity and that men have to endure more calamities in proportion as they forsake the true religion. The thesis is that of Lactantius in

*De morte persecutorum*, but amplified, and it is particularly significant as having been written immediately after the fall of Rome, thus betraying some courage in the author. Orosius' learning is often at fault, and in all that relates to ancient history he depends on his predecessors, but for the contemporary period he is a most valuable witness. The work had a great influence; copied and re-copied during the Middle Ages, it formed a basis for the first modern theories of the philosophy of history. Bossuet has taken and developed its ideas in his *Discours sur l'Histoire universelle*.

During his stay in Palestine Orosius witnessed, if not the actual discovery of the body of S. Stephen, the excitement caused by that discovery, and on leaving for the West his countryman, Avitus of Bracara, gave him a portion of the relics. Orosius left these at Minorca, where they worked miracles which converted many Jews, and the bishop, Severus, wrote an account of them in an encyclical letter: *De virtutibus ad conversionem Judæorum in Minoricensi Insula factis*. The same thing happened at Uzalis and we have already mentioned the little book written on that occasion.

The last name to be cited among S. Augustine's disciples is Leporius. This monk, who seems to have belonged originally to the diocese of Treves, owed his return to orthodoxy to the Bishop of Hippo. In 420 he held certain Christological errors, and may perhaps have shared the opinions of Pelagius. Thanks to S. Augustine he retracted in a *Libellus emendationis seu satisfactionis*, and the bishops of Africa hastened to communicate the good news to their colleagues in Gaul, in a letter that is still extant.

The above hasty review is far from exhausting

## THE FIRST SIX CENTURIES

Augustine's direct influence. We shall meet later with some of his other disciples. All those we have mentioned were his friends. They have their places here on account of their writings, for the rôle of the literary historian is to notice those only who have been writers—a fact which our readers should remember.

# THIRD PERIOD
## THE BARBARIAN TIMES
(430-636)

## SUMMARY

In the history of literature it is only by an arbitrary arrangement that S. Augustine's death marks the end of a period. The great Bishop of Hippo may be said to have long survived himself and for some years the Christian writers of the West are, so to speak, tested by his name and works. They are either for Augustine or against him. His opinions are approved or opposed. Southern Gaul, especially, is the theatre of obstinate combats in which S. Prosper on one side, SS. Cassian and Vincent of Lérins on the other, are the protagonists.

Nevertheless the Barbarian period began with S. Augustine's death. The invasion of Africa by the Vandals indicated the definitive helplessness of the Empire to defend her most indispensable possessions. Henceforth the invaders are the masters, and before them Roman civilization must retire.

One great consequence of the Barbarian victories was the formation of increasingly divergent nationalities. The unity of the Empire ensured unity of thought, and with its disappearance the ethnical groups that composed it recovered their own individuality. Formerly there was a Roman literature which could be studied without considering the nationality of the writers. Henceforth there will be an African, an Italian, a Gallic and a Spanish litera-

## THE CHRISTIAN LATIN LITERATURE

ture, and account must be taken of the countries of the last prose writers and poets of antiquity. Each of these is interested in his own little *patria*. Sometimes they deplore the fate of *Romania*, even if they do not, with Salvianus, sing the praises of the Barbarians; but that done, they are occupied with local events. Victor of Vita relates the persecution of the Vandals, Gregory of Tours writes the history of the Franks, and S. Isidore of Seville that of the Suevi and the Visigoths. The language itself gradually changes, in spite of all efforts to preserve the traditions of classical purity; it is surprising to find in S. Gregory's *History* so many forms and turns of speech that approach to the French, or at least, to the Romance language.

The great events of these troubled centuries naturally determine to some extent the character of their literature. Whether the thoughts of men turn to the past with regret or to the present with sorrow, they need consolation and encouragement. Both can be found in history, showing forth as it does the providential guidance of God; in the ascetical works that direct souls towards the hope of the heavenly Kingdom, and in the homilies and sermons reminding them of the humble duties of daily life. There are also poets, who, not without talent, express in verse the sufferings and hopes of their contemporaries, and these, especially, give evidence of a spirit of idealism.

## CHAPTER XI

### AUGUSTINISM

I. Saint Prosper. II. Saint Cassian. III. The Lérinians. IV. Other Writers. V. Saint Leo the Great.

S. AUGUSTINE's doctrines on grace and predestination, which he had formulated in his campaign against Pelagianism, found many zealous defenders, but also very determined opponents. Even before his death the controversy had begun, and it was to continue for many years, especially in Southern Gaul, which then became the intellectual centre of the West, and produced a large amount of polemical literature that is not without interest.

We find the first traces of a systematic opposition to Augustine's teaching in 428 or 429. In fact the Bishop was at that time warned by two correspondents in the south of Gaul, of the opposition that was being raised to some of his assertions. S. Augustine replied to Hilary and Prosper by sending them the required explanations, in *De prædestinatione sanctorum* and *De dono perseveratione*. We have nothing of Hilary's but his letter to S. Augustine. S. Prosper's literary career was longer.

### 1. *Saint Prosper*

Tiro Prosper was born in Aquitaine, but at the time of his correspondence with Augustine he was at Marseilles, living as an ascetic with some monks of the town. After the death of the Bishop of Hippo he went to Rome with his friend Hilary to obtain from Pope Celestine I a condemnation of semi-Pelagianism. His journey was not wholly successful, which, however, on his return to Gaul, did not prevent his continuing with renewed ardour the combat in defence of Augustine's most pronounced affirmations. When S. Leo was raised to the Pontificate Prosper returned to Rome and apparently remained there till his death in 463. He there filled important offices in the Chancery, and tradition attributes to him the editing of S. Leo's letter against Eutyches. But he found time for the discussion of the questions he had so greatly at heart and remained to the end a firm upholder of Augustinism.

Prosper employed both prose and verse in defence of his master's theories. Before Augustine's death he had found time to write to a certain Rufinus a letter on grace and free-will, a book of Epigrams against a detractor of S. Augustine, and, above all, a poem, *De Ingratis*, in which, with a play on the double meaning of the word *gratia*, he accuses the Pelagians and semi-Pelagians of ingratitude towards God. Nothing can be more austere than the subject of this poem, with its theological discussions, but Prosper succeeds in giving wonderful life to his work, making it animated and even in parts passionate, so that it is one of the most successful pieces of Christian didactic verse.

After 430 the dispute becomes more bitter as the Augustinian doctrines find a greater number of opponents in the convents of Southern Gaul. Prosper is arrested by no obstacles; one after

## THE FIRST SIX CENTURIES

another he publishes, in defence of Augustine: *Responsiones ad capitula Gallorum*, to his Gallic calumniators; to the Vincentians *Ad capitula objectionum Vincentianarum responsiones*; and to the priests at Genoa, *Pro Augustino responsiones ad excerpta Genuensium*. He even has the courage to attack Cassian in *De gratia Dei et libero arbitrio; liber contracollatorum*. About 450 he published the *Sententiæ ex Augustine delibatæ*, a collection of extracts from S. Augustine's writings, and an *Expositio psalmonum*, of which only a portion remains, seems to have been chiefly taken from Augustine's work.

Besides his polemical works, Prosper also composed a *Chronicle*, which had three editions, between 433 to 455. This Chronicle is an abridgment of S. Jerome's down to the year 378; after that date it is an independent account and acquires considerable value, particularly for the period of the author's lifetime.

Should we attribute to Prosper a book bearing the title *De vocatione omnium gentium?* This book mitigates in some degree the severity of S. Augustine's doctrine; it was certainly written in Rome under S. Leo's Pontificate and is very probably Prosper's work. If so, it is evidence of how, under the great Pope's influence, the fiery Aquitanian was induced to soften the expression of his views. But such softening must not be exaggerated. The *De vocatione* remains a wholly Augustinian work, in spite of its being a manifesto of peace.

# THE CHRISTIAN LATIN LITERATURE OF

## II. Saint Cassian

In constituting himself the champion of the Bishop of Hippo Prosper showed real courage, for in his native Provence, where he had lived for so long, the opposition to S. Augustine's doctrine was almost unanimous. The monks of Marseilles and Lérins were certainly not Pelagians, but they held that the great Doctor ascribed too small a place to man's free-will and that his ideas on predestination, on the *massa damnationis*, etc., were not solidly supported by tradition. They were not singular in this opinion; S. Augustine found many antagonists, even in Italy, and certain views of his have never been accepted by the Church.

The first to come forward in the attack was Cassian. According to Gennadius he was a Scythian by birth, but this is quite uncertain. After having spent some years in a monastery, first at Bethlehem, then in Egypt and Constantinople, where he was ordained deacon by S. John Chrysostom, he arrived at Marseilles, where he founded the celebrated monastery of S. Victor. He was its first Abbot and died there about 435.

His chief writings are in defence of the cenobitic life, of which he was the real founder in Gaul. The *De institutis Cœnobiorum et de octo principalium vitiorum remediis* treats of the rules of monastic life and of the means that should be used by the monks in combating the eight principal vices. The *Collationes*, or Conferences, contain a record of the conversations held by Cassian with the great solitaries of Egypt and show how it is possible to imitate their virtues. In this work the writer is naturally drawn to speak of free-will and its rôle in moral questions, and here he defends the semi-Pelagian opinions. S. Prosper wrote against him, but this did not prevent Cassian's work from meeting with great success among the ascetics. It was not only edited and abridged by S. Eucherius of Lyons, but in addition obtained the extraordinary honour of being translated into Greek.

Cassian's authority in the West became so great that, on the first outbreak of Nestorianism, S. Leo, then Archdeacon of Rome, requested him to write a refutation of the errors of Nestorius. The *De Incarnatione Domini contra Nestorium*, finished before the end of the summer of 430, is the first Latin work that expounds systematically the doctrine of the Incarnation. It seems to have been written hurriedly, and is, in consequence, inferior to the author's previous works.

### III. The Lérinians

Not far from Marseilles stands the monastery of Lérins, founded at the beginning of the fifth century by S. Honoratus, who became Bishop of Arles in 406. For many years Lérins was the nursery of the most remarkable bishops and writers of Southern Gaul, and was at the same time the centre of anti-Augustinian activities. Amongst its chief members were S. Eucherius of Lyons, brother of S. Honoratus, and the author of some ascetic works: *De laude Eremi; Epistola parænetica de contemptu mundi; Formularium spiritualis intelligentiæ ad Verunium; Institutiones ad Salonium;* an account of the passion of the martyrs of

Agaunum, and some homilies, of which some may have been preserved. Salonius of Geneva, the son of Eucherius, was the author of some *Mystical Explanations* on Proverbs and Ecclesiastes. S. Hilary of Arles wrote the Life of his predecessor, S. Honoratus, and a number of homilies; Valerianus of Cimiez, whose twenty homilies and a letter to the monks we still possess; S. Lupus of Troyes, whose correspondence has almost entirely disappeared; and, above all, " the mysterious Vincent of Lérins."

This latter, whose life is almost completely unknown, died at Lérins before 450, and was the author of two *Commonitoria*, intended to fix the rules of orthodoxy. Only one of these little books has been preserved: it is very short, without great originality, a good deal inspired by Tertullian and S. Augustine, but forcibly written, with incisive formulas that could be easily committed to memory. Few Christian books have attained such popularity. Often copied and still more often re-edited, the *Commonitorium* is one of the Church's great classics. The opinions it expresses, particularly on the development of dogma, appear to have obtained a right to be quoted in theology. S. Vincent is, nevertheless, clearly opposed to the Augustinian theses, and Prosper wrote against him. However, his opposition to the opinions of the great Bishop of Hippo does not seem to have affected his success.

### IV. *Other Writers*

It was not only in Gaul that S. Augustine's writings were attacked. Amongst his most violent

## THE FIRST SIX CENTURIES

opponents was the author of the anonymous treatise known as the *Prædestinatus*. This work, after giving a list of all the ancient heresies, denounces a new error called Predestinarianism. The exposure of this heresy takes up the whole of the second book, and the third contains a detailed refutation. It is generally admitted that the *Prædestinatus* was written in Rome, under the Pontificate of Sixtus III (432-440), and that it reflects the opinions then current in the capital of the Christian world. Can we go further and name the author of this disturbing work? Dom Morin attributes the preface, the first and the third book to Arnobius the younger, maintaining, however, that the second book is the work of an avowed Predestinarian.

This does not tell us much, for we know almost nothing of Arnobius himself. He was probably a monk living in Rome, in the middle of the fifth century. His literary work appears to have been extensive; he wrote some *Commentarii in Psalmos*, with allegorical explanations, which are not without interest for the history of doctrine, and the rather banal *Expositiunculæ in Evangelium*. Dom Morin also attributes to him a curious *Conflictus Arnobii catholici cum Serapione Aegyptio*, a dialogue directed against Monophysitism, and in which, strangely enough, S. Augustine's authority is upheld. He is also the author of a *Libellus ad Gregoriam*, addressed to a great Roman lady and full of wise and moderate counsels. It is, however, possible that Arnobius' literary legacy is not so great as Dom Morin believes. In any case it is interesting from its variety and by the light it casts on the Roman monastic world of 450, which enables us to measure the distance traversed by the ascetics of the capital since the days when S. Jerome reproached them so caustically for their quarrelsome and vagabond habits.

Of the predecessors of S. Leo we possess only letters: thirty-six of Innocent I; sixteen of Zosimus; nine of Boniface I; sixteen of Celestine I, and eight of Sixtus III. All these letters are invaluable for the historian, but of less importance as literature, although most of them are written in the clear firm style of the Roman Curia. They show that a tradition of nobility, majesty and simplicity had already been formed and that the pontifical Chancery possessed, or at least was on the point of possessing, its own rules. In the midst of the Barbarians the Roman Church preserves the Empire's inheritance, including its respect for literary form and the classic tongue.

### V. Saint Leo the Great

History has given the title of " Great " to S. Leo, the successor of Pope Sixtus III, and none has more truly deserved it. His Pontificate of one-and-twenty years (440-461) was passed in a most critical period. The Eastern Church was troubled by the heresies of Nestorius and Eutyches and agitated by the demands of the Patriarch of Constantinople: the Church of the West was disturbed by survivals of Manichæism and Priscillianism, and, more than all, the ancient Empire was being utterly destroyed. The Barbarians ravaged Italy from north to south, the hordes of Attila appeared at the gates of Rome and Genseric's soldiery pillaged the Eternal City. Nevertheless life had to go on, urgent problems had to be solved, anxious souls reassured and many

## THE FIRST SIX CENTURIES

other matters decided. S. Leo was equal to everything. In face of the most threatening dangers he maintained the unshaken tranquillity of a valiant soul. His calm won the admiration of Attila, his steadfastness triumphed over Genseric's cruelty. When the Monophysite heresy crept in from the East his clear intellect discovered a formula that rendered the poison ineffective and expressed the belief of the Catholic Church. To the throne of S. Peter he brought the majesty of a Roman emperor. More than this: in the midst of the ruin caused by the Barbarian invasions and by the very weakness of those who should have upheld her, S. Leo proclaimed the eternal glory of Rome, more powerful than ever through the triumph of the Church. The Popes who preceded him had never ignored the authority they held from Christ, through the Apostolical succession; S. Leo became, as it were, their voice: in their name he proclaimed to the world the primacy of the Holy See, and not content with proclaiming it, he exercised that primacy on every occasion.

The letters which bear S. Leo's name are not all his, and some must have been drawn up by his Chancery. The most important is that addressed to Flavian—the sublime dogmatic Epistle which condemned the heresy of Eutyches and defined the true Catholic Faith in the Incarnation. This decree was accepted by the council of Chalcedon. The other letters are more particularly interesting to history and theology.

His sermons appeal to the lettered: they are mostly short, but in design and style are of remarkable purity. Whether he treats of moral subjects or dogmatic questions, S. Leo always expresses himself as a master. Exact words, sonorous phrases, where the antithesis often serves to bring out the fundamental idea into stronger relief, a great regard for form, euphony and rhythm, such are the qualities that recommend these homilies to the cultured and make the collection one of the most remarkable models of Christian preaching.

Is S. Leo the author of the so-called *Sacramentarium Leonianum*? It is uncertain, though the collection is ancient and some of the prayers remind us of the great Pope's homilies. The book should be mentioned here as one of the first liturgical works of the Roman Church, and an admirable specimen of the brief yet forcible style that characterizes the official prayers of Roman Catholicism.

By the side of S. Leo two contemporary Italian bishops must be mentioned, who did their best to second him in his defence of orthodoxy and preaching of the rule of morals. These are S. Peter Chrysologus, Bishop of Ravenna, and S. Maximus, Bishop of Turin. S. Peter has left us only a letter to Eutyches and some homilies, intentionally short, written in a familiar style, where antitheses, proverbs and effective phrases are not wanting: they are a good example of popular preaching in the fifth century.

S. Maximus has also left sermons, very similar in their qualities and defects to those of S. Chrysologus. The works of these two writers have been very little studied, and so far we possess no critical edition. It is, however, certain that much that is apocryphal is mixed with genuine matter, and that a serious examination of these collections is a necessary duty for scholars: quite recently it has been found that several homilies attributed to

## THE FIRST SIX CENTURIES

S. Maximus are really the work of the Arian Maximinus. SS. Peter and Maximus were much appreciated by their contemporaries and even more so by their successors. The very surname of "Chrysologus" bestowed on S. Peter testifies to the veneration rendered to his memory. To-day we are less moved by their not very original eloquence, which seems to have been that of zealous bishops rather than of superior talent.

## CHAPTER XII

### THE LAST POETS OF ANTIQUITY

I. Gallic Poets. II. Sidonius Apollinaris. III. Sedulius and Dracontius. IV. Saint Avitus and Ennodius. V. Fortunatus.

WHILST the Barbarians were completing their invasion of the Empire and destroying the last remains of the ancient civilization, some poets of distinction were endeavouring to save at least something from the ruins and to forget the misfortunes of the time in singing the praises of God and recalling to the faithful the duties of Christian life. Nearly all these last poets of the Latin world are of Gallic origin and most of their writings are didactic compositions, the themes being taken from the Bible or traditional preaching. They therefore all belong to the same spiritual type, or, more exactly, to one same group of Christian society.

### I. Gallic Poets

Under the title of *S. Paulini Epigramma* we possess a lively satire of Gallo-Roman manners about the year 400. It consists of one hundred and ten hexameters, in the form of a dialogue, and is written in

## THE CHRISTIAN LATIN LITERATURE

easy and flowing language. It is ascribed to Bishop Paulinus of Beziers, who, according to the Chronicle of Hydatius, was also the author of an encyclical letter, now lost.

The manuscript containing the *Epigramma* also gives us the text of a long poem in three books, called *Alethia* and attributed to a certain Claudius Marius Victor, *Orator Massaliensis*. Thanks to Gennadius we know that this writer lived in the fifth century and wrote a Commentary in verse on Genesis as far as the death of Abraham. We do not possess a complete commentary, for in its present state *Alethia* concludes with the destruction of Sodom and Gomorrha. The author tells us in the Prologue that his book is intended for the instruction of youth and therefore he omits some of the Biblical narratives. Those he relates are expressed in verses of classic workmanship, full of Virgilian and similar ideas. Occasionally a spirit of true poetry breathes in the verses and animates some of the episodes, and we certainly find in Victor a very distinguished mind.

The Bishop Orientius of Auch was the contemporary of Marius Victor. His life is known to us from the accounts given in the *Acta Sanctorum* of the Bollandists. His literary work is confined to a *Commonitorium* in two books, intended to teach the reader " by what means we may open heaven and put evil to flight." It therefore conveys a moral lesson, and it is in fact a series of counsels on practical life that Orientius presents to his readers in this long poem of elegiac couplets. There is conviction in this long sermon which sometimes uplifts the author, but power is wanting, and we have to content ourselves with discovering, in the always correct verses, the many classical reminiscences that attest the writer's solid education.

Paulinus of Pella was the grandson of Ausonius; though born in Macedonia, he belongs to Gaul by family tradition and almost his whole life. He has himself related his extraordinarily troubled life, in a poem written at the age of eighty-three, which he calls *Eucharisticos*, in thanksgiving for the many favours God had bestowed on him. The greatest of these was, without doubt, the preservation of his life. For Paulinus had been through the Barbarian invasions; he had seen the Goths and Alani pillage Aquitaine; he had lost all his goods; he had witnessed the successive deaths of his mother-in-law, his mother, his wife and one of his sons. Ruined and alone, he nevertheless finds strength to praise God, and he praises Him with great simplicity and true feeling, in spite of some affectation of style and too many classical allusions. The *Eucharisticos* is a curious testimony of that troubled period, as well as the confession of a beautiful soul.

Paulinus of Perigueux is not, like his namesake of Pella, crushed by the troubles of the times. The holy Bishop walks rather in the footsteps of Sulpicius Severus, and seventy years after the latter becomes a fresh panegyrist of S. Martin of Tours. The long poem in six books that he composed in honour of the great thaumaturgist is in fact a versified adaptation of the *Life* and the *Dialogues* of Sulpicius, and of a more recent work on the Saint's last miracles by Bishop Perpetuus of Tours. Having finished his book Paulinus completed his work by writing a metrical inscription for the new basilica at Tours and by an account of the miraculous cure of one of his grandsons. Needless to add, there is nothing striking in all this poetry. It is the work of an honest versifier who knew his trade and applied its rules, and Paulinus probably ambitioned no other glory than that.

## II. *Sidonius Apollinaris*

A more interesting figure is that of Sidonius Apollinaris, born in Lyons in 431 or 432. He died at Clermont-Ferrand in 498. His career also was one of many vicissitudes, and nothing is more characteristic of those barbarous times than the life of this great Gallo-Roman lord, whose support was sought by all the usurpers and who pronounced successive panegyrics on the Emperors Avitus, Majorian and Anthemius. He became prefect of Rome and ended his career as Bishop of Clermont in Auvergne, after having, not without difficulty, gained the good graces of the Arian Visigoths. In all this there must have been a good deal of recantation,[1] but one can hardly judge him harshly, considering the circumstances. We must also remember that Sidonius' life divides itself in two; before he became a bishop he was only a rich and influential proprietor, who devoted his leisure hours to literature, and whose great delight was to write a fine letter or learned poem. He excelled in compositions for special occasions; imperial panegyrics, descriptions of towns and castles, epithalamia, petitions, letters of thanks and the like, all matters of a day. He improves his verse, polishes his style and recalls his classic mythology to adorn his

[1] *Beaucoup de palinodies.*

writings. He is admired by all his contemporaries, and he knows it; his correspondents are distinguished members of Roman society, and his letters are full of hyperbole and flattery; in a word, he makes every effort to avoid simplicity. Then comes, quite unexpectedly, the episcopate. Sidonius almost gives up poetry; his letters become grave and serious; the time of badinage is passed, the Bishop must devote himself to his new duties, and he did this so completely that posterity has venerated him as a Saint. When to-day we read his works, twenty-four poems and nine books of letters, we seek first for a vivid picture of the history of the time, and few documents are more instructive; then we look for the remains of Latin culture, still living in the midst of the Barbarians, and it is a pleasing surprise to find them so numerous.

### III. *Sedulius and Dracontius*

Leaving Gaul for the moment, we meet first with Sedulius, who wrote between 425 and 450, but whose life is unknown to us. He was at any rate a true poet who took the Gospel for his guide. The four last books of his *Carmen Paschale* are dedicated to the praise of the miracles of Christ, the first being a sort of introduction containing a summary of the miracles in the Old Testament. S. Matthew is his chief guide, though he does not neglect the other Evangelists and even draws occasionally on S. Ambrose and S. Augustine's Commentaries.

The *Carmen* was addressed to a friend, the priest Macedonius, who seems not to have been quite satisfied with it, and at his request Sedulius translated his poem into prose. This, at least, is the best explanation one can give of the *Opus Paschale*, and it was an unfortunate experiment: Sedulius' prose is more obscure, entangled and pompous than his verse. The *Opus* is a mass of periphrases and accumulation of metaphors in the worst possible taste.

Two hymns complete Sedulius' work; the first, consisting of fifty-five distichs, in which the promises of the Old Testament are paralleled with their realization in the New, are a fatiguing *jeu d'esprit*. The second hymn, on the contrary, of twenty-three strophes in iambic dimeter, contains some really beautiful verses, and the Church has borrowed two fragments in her liturgy for Christmas and the Epiphany.

Sedulius was certainly an Italian. Dracontius belonged to Africa, having been born and lived at Carthage during the second half of the fifth century. After a brilliant career he was unfortunate enough to rouse the anger of the Vandal King, Gonthamond (484-496), who threw him into prison. There he gave up writing mythological poetry, which he had hitherto cultivated with success, and his sufferings having led him to serious reflection, he composed a *Satisfactio*, addressed to Gonthamond, imploring his pardon. This touching prayer, eloquently invoking the Divine Mercy, met with no response. Without further insisting, Dracontius undertook a fresh work: the *Laudes Dei*, in three books, in which he praises the goodness of God to man. The Creation and the Incarnation are the themes of the first two books, and the third consists of invitations to the exercise of gratitude and love to so good a God. In this poem we behold the writer's true qualities.

The language is often barbarous, and the rhythm leaves much to be desired, but it has spring, power and enthusiasm. Its defects are those of the time and are irremediable, but its good qualities belong to Dracontius and show real talent.

### IV. Saint Avitus and Ennodius

We must return to Gaul to study the last poets of the Patristic period. Avitus of Vienne, Ennodius of Pavia and Fortunatus of Poitiers were all three bishops, for the episcopate was at that time the last refuge of civilization.

Alcimus Ecdicius Avitus, born at Vienne in Dauphiny, in 450, or thereabouts, was elected Bishop of his native town in 490 and died about 518. He held an important place in the religious history of his time, for he converted the Burgundian King Sigismund to Catholic orthodoxy; he fought vigorously against heresy, especially Arianism and Eutychianism; he restored ecclesiastical discipline; he upheld the Pope's authority, and he occupied himself actively with the many problems that arose in an epoch that was so fertile in surprising events.

He holds no less a position in literary history, for he was a prolific writer, both in verse and in prose. His prose works include two books: *Contra Eutychianam Haeresim*, and *Dialogi cum Gundobado Rege*; about a hundred letters that are historically of great importance; two homilies on the Rogations, and some fragments of sermons.

## THE FIRST SIX CENTURIES

The style of all these writings is lax and the language barbarous: a mournful testimony to the misery of the time. But we are happily surprised when we open Avitus' poetic works, for there are to be found some reminiscences of the classics. On one side is the spoken tongue, with all its faults; on the other the language written by the cultured classes who endeavour to follow classic models.

The most important of the poetic works is the *Libelli de Spiritalis Historiæ Gestis*, which is divided into five books: the Beginning of the World, Original Sin, the Judgment of God, the Deluge and the Passage of the Red Sea. Like many of his predecessors Avitus draws his inspiration from the Bible, but he does not want originality, and the three first books in particular, where Original Sin forms the central idea, contain many happy developments. The 666 hexameters of the *De Consolatoria Castitatis Laude*, addressed to the poet's sister, are not so new or interesting. Avitus composed many other poems. He tells us that he had intended to make a collection of them, but that in the sack of Vienne, he had lost them nearly all. This little piece of information, told, as it were, in passing, in the dedicatory prologue to the *Spiritual History*, enlightens us on the conditions under which the poets of that time had to write.

Though Magnus Felix Ennodius was born in Gaul about 473, he spent most of his life in Italy. After finishing his studies in Milan, where he spent some time as a professor of rhetoric, he became Bishop of Pavia in 513 and died in 521. He was a polygraph of the most astonishing sort and one of the last representatives of an empty and solemn rhetoric. His 297 letters are little more than scholastic exer-

## THE CHRISTIAN LATIN LITERATURE OF

cises, *Controversiæ* on the ancient models: affected and far-fetched, they are worthless except for the attempts at virtuosity they manifest. The *Opuscula* are more interesting; amongst these should be mentioned an emphatic and exaggerated panegyric of Theodoric, a *Libellus adversus eos qui contra Synodum scribere præsumpserunt* (he refers to the Roman council of 502); a *Life* of S. Epiphanius of Pavia, one of his predecessors; a *Life* of S. Antony of Lérins; a *Eucharisticon de Vita sua;* a *Parænesis didascalica*, which is a sort of manual of rhetoric. About thirty discourses, where the profane and the sacred are strangely mingled, and two books of poems complete the work of Ennodius. The poems are various in character; there are some hymns in honour of Christ, epigrams which remind one of Martial, inscriptions for churches, tombs and paintings. There is no great art in all these: they are the laborious compositions of a good pupil of rhetoric who strives to imitate his masters and to preserve their traditions in spite of the growing barbarism around him.

### V. Fortunatus

The wandering life of Venanantius Honorius Fortunatus rouses our interest in his personality. Born near Treviso, in Upper Italy, and educated at Ravenna, Fortunatus was cured of a disease of the eyes through the intercession of S. Martin of Tours, and thereupon undertook a pilgrimage of thanksgiving to the Saint's tomb. This pilgrimage, however, gave him the opportunity of visiting other countries and seeing the world. To reach Tours

## THE FIRST SIX CENTURIES

he crossed the Julian Alps, Norica and Rhaetia, and visited other places. He saw many things along his route and made many friends. In order to gain a livelihood he sang as the troubadours would do later; he wrote many pleasing little verses on the gods and goddesses of mythology; he multiplied poems in praise of his friends and patrons. At Metz, where he arrived at the time of King Sigebert's marriage with Brunehild, he composed an Epithalamium for the occasion. After satisfying his devotion at the tomb of S. Martin, he crossed the Pyrenees and then reached Poitiers. Here he met S. Radegunde; a providential meeting that caused the wanderer to settle. Radegunde was attracted by Fortunatus and made him her secretary; he devoted himself to the saintly Queen, who had taken the veil and was then living in her monastery at Poitiers, and whose piety and almsgiving Fortunatus admired. She had been dead about ten years when, finally, our troubadour became a priest, and on the death of Plato, Bishop of Poitiers, Fortunatus was elected to succeed him, in 597. He died early in the following century.

Perhaps we may say that he did not wholly die, for he left many writings in which his charming personality has survived. They are not great works, but pleasing and facile, showing great talent. His prose writings are biographies: that of S. Hilary of Poitiers, accompanied and supplemented by an account of the Saint's miracles; of S. Albinus of Angers, S. Germanus of Paris, S. Paternus of Avranches, S. Marcellus of Paris, S. Serinus of Bordeaux, and above all, of his holy patroness, S. Radegunde. All these *Lives* are con-

structed on classical models and contain eulogies rather than history. There is, however, enough of the latter to make the books of value, and they also contain some interesting literary developments.
Fortunatus' poetic works are more varied, and it is these that have assured his fame. The most important, by its length, is the *Life of S. Martin*, containing no less than 2,243 hexameters, but it is neither the best nor the most interesting. After Sulpicius Severus and Paulinus of Perigueux there is not much matter left for another writer. Fortunatus wrote at the request of Gregory of Tours, but does not appear to have undertaken the task with much enthusiasm, for he finished it within two months.

The other pieces are shorter. They are mostly occasional verses; letters, elegies, epithalamia, consolations, panegyrics, inscriptions, etc.; the "small change" of a poet obliged to gain his livelihood and satisfy the vanity of an insatiable clientèle. These little trifles are valuable only for their elegance; we can set aside the matter; the form is pleasing and shows real talent. Occasionally the subject itself rises to a higher level, and then we have poems worthy of all praise. Such are the verses on the destruction of Thuringia, and much more the two hymns on the Passion: *Vexilla Regis prodeunt*, and *Pange lingua gloriosi*. These hymns have become part of the liturgy, and they remain as a witness to the writer's faith and his devotion to his crucified Lord.

Fortunatus is the last representative, in poetry, of classic art; his language is already full of barbarisms, of which he accuses himself and humbly begs his readers' pardon. No doubt there were

## THE FIRST SIX CENTURIES

writers in prose and verse after his time, and history records no brusque interruption, or total cessation followed by an unexpected renewal. But the successors of Fortunatus belong to the Middle Ages and do not concern us here.

# CHAPTER XIII

### BARBARIAN AND BYZANTINE AFRICA

I. The Barbarian Period. II. Byzantine Controversies.

THE Vandals, called into Africa by Count Boniface, were not long in making war on their own account. By 439 the greater portion of the Roman province was in their hands, and a few years later they completed its conquest without effort. The Vandals were Arians, and under Genseric and Hunneric they made life hard for the Catholics. Persecutions and martyrdoms began again. Christian literature suffered under these tragic conditions: whilst the theologians tried to uphold the true Faith of Nicæa against the Arians the historians and chroniclers related the sorrowful events of which they were the witnesses or the victims.

### *I. The Barbarian Period*

Several distinguished themselves in the Arian controversy: S. Eugenius of Carthage (480-505), who drew up the profession of Faith read in the assembly of 484 and wrote a letter to his fellow-citizens encouraging them to keep the Catholic

# THE CHRISTIAN LATIN LITERATURE

Faith; Cerealis of Castellum in Cæsarian Mauretania, the author of a short work against the Arian Maximinus; Antoninus Honoratus of Cirta in Numidia, from whom we have a touching letter of encouragement to Arcadius; Asclepas; Victor of Cartenna; Voconius of Castellum; of these last the writings mentioned by Gennadius have been lost.

A separate place must be given to Vigilius of Thapsus and Fulgentius of Ruspe, the two great theologians of this troubled period. Of Vigilius, Bishop of Thapsus in Byzacene, we only know that he took part in the Conference of February, 484. The rest of his life is unknown and the list of his works is uncertain. A book *Against the Arian Maribadus* and another *Against the Arian Palladius* are lost. The *Dialogue* against the Arians, the Sabellians, and the Photinians, and the five books *Against Eutyches* are certainly genuine. But the other writings sometimes ascribed to him, and in particular the twelve books *On the Trinity*, do not seem to be his.

S. Fulgentius of Ruspe is better known to us and his rôle is more considerable. His troubled life is characteristic of the times in which he lived. Formed, it would seem, for a life of solitude and peace, he is jostled about and faced with some of the greatest problems a man of action may have to solve.

Born at Telepte in Byzacene in 468 he early developed an attraction for the ascetic life; he lived as a monk in Africa in the midst of great difficulties, sometimes persecuted by the Arians, at others troubled by the Moors. He tried unsuccessfully to go into Egypt; after a pilgrimage to Rome he returned to Africa, where he founded a monastery, but was soon sought out to be made Bishop of Ruspe, and thus, against his will, brought into public life. Though very soon exiled to Sardinia, his knowledge and talents pointed him out as the spokesman of his colleagues. He wrote much, not only against Arianism, but also against Pelagianism, semi-Pelagianism and the Eutychians: he interested himself in all the theological questions of his time: he was *the* great man of Western Christendom, the oracle consulted by the Catholic Church. Recalled from his first exile in 515, he did not finally return to Ruspe till 523. For another ten years he ruled his little diocese, and edified his flock by his austere life, whilst continuing his writing; his works were spread, not only over Africa, but in Rome and throughout the entire West.

Many of his works, and perhaps the most important, are connected with the Arian controversy. In 515 he had been challenged by the King Thrasimund to answer certain questions raised by the Arians: the books *Contra Arianos* and *Ad Trasimundum Regem Vandalorum libri tres* were the Saint's replies. A work, *Adversus Pintam*, and a *Commonitorium* on the Holy Ghost belong to the same period as Fulgentius. The following books seem to be later: *De Trinitate*, to the notary Felix; *Against the Discourse of the Arian Fastidiosus*; *On the Incarnation of the Son of God*; *Against the Arian Fabianus*.

Other of Fulgentius' works concern the questions of grace, which, since the time of S. Augustine, had not ceased to exercise the minds of many. Fulgentius here shows himself as the faithful disciple of the great Doctor, and in defence of his doctrine he composed two books: *De remissione peccatorum*, three books *Ad Maximum*; seven *Contra Faustum*. Then, after his return to Africa, three books *De veritate prædestinationis et gratiæ Dei*, and an encyclical letter to John and Venerius.

Whilst he was in Sardinia some Scythian monks questioned him on the Incarnation, and in reply he wrote an important treatise, *On the Incarnation and Grace*, but it is clear from what he says that the formula of the Eastern monks which had given rise to their questions: *Unus de Trinitate passus est in carne*, did not interest him much, and he used the opportunity to expound his views on grace.

A small work, *De Fide*, some letters and discourses complete Fulgentius' literary work. During his lifetime he enjoyed a great reputation, which has been sanctioned by succeeding centuries. We are to-day inclined to be more severe on this methodical mind, this clear but rather shallow intellect, with his correct but uninspired style. But we must guard ourselves against too great severity in judging this contemporary of the Vandal kings. In fact, Fulgentius is much above the other African bishops of that time and deserves the admiration bestowed on him by his biographer, Fulgentius Ferrandus.

The latter became a deacon of Carthage in 523, and besides the Life of S. Fulgentius we possess some of his letters and a *Breviatio Canonum Ecclesiasticorum*, which summarizes in 232 canons the teachings of the African and Greek councils and is one of the first attempts at canonical codification.

Whilst Vigilius of Thapse multiplied *Apologies* for the Catholic Faith against the victorious Arians, Victor of Vita, another African bishop, wrote a history of the persecution of which he was himself one of the victims. This *History* relates in three books the calamities of the Church of Africa between 429 and 484. The first book, which covers the reign of Genseric to 477, is drawn from foreign sources; in the following two Victor writes as an eye-witness and an actor in the horrors he relates. He tells of what he has seen and suffered, in company with his fellow bishops, and he does this with deep emotion. He still has before his eyes the horrible scenes he has witnessed; he still hears the cries of joy of the persecutors and the groans of their victims. The work, of great value for history, is also remarkable from a literary point of view. Victor possesses the rare gift of narration; in spite of his often barbarous language, or perhaps on account of it, his work is one of extraordinary power.

## II. Byzantine Controversies

During the last years of the Vandal occupation the African bishops had been called upon to advise on questions raised by the Eastern theologians. When, in 533, Africa was reconquered by Belisarius and became again a province of the Byzantine empire, her bishops had naturally to take a more active part in these controversies. Justinian then occupied the imperial throne, and gave all the time he could spare from politics to the study of theology. He did not fear to give work to Councils, and found sometimes that the African Church decided against the decisions made by the synods he convoked.

This was clearly shown during the course of the

## THE FIRST SIX CENTURIES

dispute about the " Three Chapters," provoked by the condemnation of the works of Theodore of Mopsuestia, Theodoret of Cyrus and Ibas. In 546 Fulgentius Ferrandus had given to the Roman deacons Anatolius and Pelagius advice that was contrary to Justinian's projected condemnation. At the same time a powerful theologian, Facundus, Bishop of Hermiane in Byzacene, who was then at Constantinople, wrote a considerable work, *In defence of the Three Chapters*, and long after the condemnation of 553, he again expressed his view in a book *Against the scholastic Mocianus* and in a *Letter on the Catholic Faith in defence of the Three Chapters*.

By the side of Facundus must be placed other African writers: Bishop Pontianus, author of a *Letter to Justinian*; Verecundus of Junca, to whom we owe *Extracts from the Acts of the Council of Chalcedon*, intended to hinder the condemnation of the Three Chapters, nine books of *Commentaries* on the ecclesiastical canticles, and a small poem in 212 hexameters, full of mistakes, *On the Satisfaction of Repentance*; and the deacon, Liberatus, who, between 560 and 570 wrote an interesting *Breviarium causæ Nestorianorum et Eutychianorum*, which summarizes the history of the two great Eastern heresies between 428 and 553.

There were other writers who, though more or less mixed up with the affair of the Three Chapters, have left no works on the subject. Such was Primasius of Hadrumetum, who, with some of his colleagues, was ordered by the emperor to repair to Constantinople to give an account of the attitude of the African episcopate. Primasius was a celebrated exegetist; we have of his a *Commentary on the Apocalypse*, not very original, borrowed chiefly from Tyconius and S. Augustine. A Commentary on the Epistles of S. Paul has often been ascribed to him, but it is certainly not his work.

Junilius, though a layman, was a friend of Primasius, and at his request wrote the *Instituta regularia divinæ Legis*, a small manual of Introduction to the study of the Bible. The writer there adopts the exegetical theories of Theodore of Mopsuestia: as the latter was at the time the object of condemnation at Constantinople, it required some little skill to defend his views without naming him.

The Chronicle had always been popular with the Africans and it continued to be so under the Byzantine domination. The last chronicler was Victor of Tunnuna, who was a victim of Justinian's resentment and died in a cloister at Constantinople. He composed an immense *Chronicle*, from the Creation to the year 566. Only the last part of this work is extant; it dates from 444 to 566 and furnishes valuable information on the history of the African Church.

None of the above are great writers; to judge them fairly we have to remember the troubled conditions under which they lived: neither the Vandal nor Byzantine governments offered favourable opportunities for the development or preservation of Latin culture in Africa. Rather it is wonderful that in such an environment men like S. Fulgentius of Ruspe or Victor of Vita should have lived. The works of these two bishops, as well as that of their contemporaries, bear admirable witness to the vitality of Roman civilization in Africa.

# CHAPTER XIV

### ITALY

I. Secondary Writers.　II. Boethius.　III. Cassiodorus. IV. Saint Gregory the Great.

IN spite of the ruin caused by the Barbarian invasions, Italy remained the privileged land of the ancient civilization. The Popes and the bishops faithfully kept up the traditions of the old Latin tongue. Few of them were great writers, but they expressed themselves with rare correctness. In the sixth century two men raised the torch on high: Boethius the layman and Cassiodorus the monk. Both belonged to ancient and noble Roman families and, following to the end the examples of their ancestors, they filled important posts in the service of the State. Both were profoundly Christian; the lustre they cast on their own century belongs to the Church, whose glory they are. Finally, in the last days of antiquity, at the dawn of the Middle Ages the Pope S. Gregory sums up, as it were, in his own person, all past history and prognosticates that which is to come: he closes magnificently the long series of great Doctors of the Latin Church.

# THE CHRISTIAN LATIN LITERATURE OF

## *I. Secondary Writers*

The first Italian writers of the fifth and sixth centuries may be passed rapidly over. Most of them possess no striking personality and their works are not of great literary value. First, there is the long series of Popes, from S. Hilary to S. Gregory: we possess their letters, important for history rather than for literature. S. Gelasius (492-496) should, however, have special mention, for in the course of his too brief Pontificate he displayed marvellous activity in putting an end to the schism which then separated the Greek from the Latin Church. Four treatises relate to this matter: the *Gesta de nomine Acacii*; the *De damnatione nominum Petri et Acacii*; the *De duabus Naturis in Christo*; and the *Tomus de Anathematis Vinculo*. A treatise against the Pelagian heresy and another against the Senator Andromachus and the other Romans who wished to celebrate the *Lupercalia* according to ancient custom, show that Gelasius busied himself not only with the schism of Acacius, but with all the interests of the West. The decree respecting the books to be approved or prohibited is no more his than is the so-called " Gelasian Sacramentary." That these two highly important works should have been attributed to him shows the reverence attached to the memory of this great Pope.

Soon after Gelasius' death the first editions of the *Liber Pontificalis* were compiled at Rome, in which the Christian public can learn the history of the early Popes. Under the Pontificate of Liberius, as we have seen, there had already been published a catalogue of the Popes, giving the length of each

## THE FIRST SIX CENTURIES

one's reign together with some more or less precise information. At the end of the sixth century this catalogue, continued and completed in various ways, still existed. It was a document of this kind that Pope Hormisdas took as the basis of a new work; the first redaction was favourable to the anti-Pope Laurentius and has entirely disappeared. Another, written in an opposite sense, has been preserved. Unfortunately it is the work of a writer little qualified to write serious history. It is a bizarre collection of information taken from reliable sources, and from legends of all kinds. From the time of Symmachus onwards the writer is more exact, but he was evidently a cleric of inferior class and writes from the point of view of a man of the people. Nevertheless the book had a great success, and the *Liber Pontificalis* is a book of capital importance for the historian of the Roman Church.

There was living in Rome at that time a learned man, a Scythian by birth, who was an honour to the world by his works on chronology and canon law. This was Dionysius Exiguus, or "The Little," a surname that he seems to have adopted out of humility. His great concern was to acquaint the Latin Christians with the legislation of the Greek councils, and to this end he published the *Collectio Dionysiana*, containing the so-called "Canons of the Apostles," then the canons of Nicæa, Ancyra, Neo-Cæsarea, Gangra, Laodicea, Constantinople, Sardis and those of the African councils. This compilation, published under Symmachus, was greatly appreciated, and Dionysius brought out two successive editions. A third, prepared under Hormisdas, comprised only the Greek councils and omitted the Canons of the

# THE CHRISTIAN LATIN LITERATURE OF

Apostles. About the same time he made a collection of papal constitutions: *Collectio decretorum Pontificum Romanorum*, from Siricius to Anastasius II. This collection of Decretals only contains thirty-nine letters, and is therefore incomplete.

To his canonical works Dionysius added Chronology. For many centuries, almost, indeed, from the beginning of Christianity, discussions on the date of Easter had been constantly renewed. The many attempts to form a Paschal Cycle that should be universally approved had been unsuccessful. Dionysius took up the study of the question and recommended to the Roman Church the adoption of the Alexandrian Cycle of nineteen years. At the same time he substituted for the " Era of Diocletian," or " of Rome," then generally used, a new era, dating from the Incarnation of the Word of God. This " Era of the Incarnation," or " Dionysian Era," is now universally employed, though Dionysius made a mistake of at least four years in the date of the Annunciation.

Chronology and history interested other writers also. The Roman deacon, John, addressed an important letter to Senarius, about the year 500, on the baptismal liturgy. A little later the Abbot Eugippius wrote the Life of S. Severinus, the apostle of Norica, and published some extracts from S. Augustine's works, which had a great circulation. Towards 535 the Illyrian, Marcellinus Comes, published a Chronicle of events between 379 and 534. About fifteen years later the historian Jordanis composed a résumé of universal history and abridged Cassiodorus' book *On the History of the Goths*. Between 581 and 593 Marius of Lausanne continued Prosper's *Chronicle* up to 581.

## THE FIRST SIX CENTURIES

All these works and many others testify to the intellectual curiosity for knowledge during the sorrowful sixth century.

However, those who desired to live a perfect life continued to retire into monasteries, and this movement received a great impetus through the influence of the celebrated Abbot of Monte Cassino, S. Benedict of Nursia, who in 529 wrote that Rule which is a perfect model of wisdom and prudence, and drew multitudes to follow him. Without literary pretension, the Benedictine Rule is a monument of Roman language and authority: it possesses all the powerful qualities of the ancient race who for so long ruled the world, and it was to perpetuate through the ages a like sovereignty over the hearts and wills of men.

### II. Boethius

Like S. Benedict, though in a very different way, Anicius Manlius Torquatus Severinus Boethius was to revive the best qualities of Rome. He belonged to the illustrious family of the Anicii, who had already given S. Paulinus of Nola to the Church. Born about 480, he rose rapidly to honourable posts; he was consul in 510, and in 522 saw his two young sons promoted to the same dignity. King Theodoric heaped favours upon him. Then, suddenly, his fortune changed. Accused of high treason, he was thrown into prison and executed between 524 and 526.

His tragic fate did not, however, take him unprepared, for Boethius had for long drunk from the purest sources of philosophy. Plato and Aristotle held no secrets for him and he had formed the vast project of translating their complete works into Latin. His sudden death prevented him from carrying this out. But he did at least translate some treatises on logic and published a certain number of Commentaries, of which the Commentary on *De Interpretatione* and those on the *Isagoge* of Porphyry are the most remarkable. It was by their means that medieval scholars learnt to know Aristotle's logic.

Boethius' fame does not, however, rest on his works on logic, but on the work he wrote in prison, the *Consolations of Philosophy*. Few ancient writings have exercised a deeper influence. A combination of prose and verse, this admirable dialogue between the author and Philosophy sets forth in all their acuteness the great problems of the sufferings of the just, of Providence, of the Sovereign Good. Problems old as the world; they are here reproduced under circumstances which naturally evoke them, for the questioner is the powerful minister of yesterday, the martyr of to-morrow. To these anxious questions Philosophy replies by counsels of peace and calm, of strength, which recall the purest teachings of ancient wisdom. But one cannot but be greatly astonished that nothing higher is spoken of, and it has been considered doubtful whether Boethius was really a Christian: how could the author of the *Consolations* be content with philosophy if he had the Faith? But it is hardly fair to put the question in this form, for there are difficulties raised by reason and which must be answered by reason: such is the problem of evil, and the believer is not forbidden to think by the fact that he has Faith. Boethius

## THE FIRST SIX CENTURIES

in prison reminds us of Socrates, but he is a Christian Socrates, and if we wish for proofs of his religion we shall find them in his theological *opuscula, On the Trinity, Against Nestorius,* and others, to the genuineness of which Cassiodorus testifies.

### III. *Cassiodorus*

He was a contemporary, a friend and a relation of Boethius, though a very different character: Boethius was speculative and philosophical, whilst Cassiodorus was a practical man, whose principal efforts were directed to the preservation of the ancient culture in the barbarian world.

Magnus Aurelius Cassiodorus Senator belonged to one of the oldest Roman families, and, like Boethius, was a favourite counsellor of Theodoric. But, more fortunate than his friend, he retained the King's favour, and for forty years rose to higher and higher official posts. Then, on the threshold of old age he threw up his career, abandoned the world and retired, in 560, to the monastery of Vivarium, which he had founded on one of his estates. Henceforth he pursued a double design: the first was, in common with the other monks, to work out his salvation; but his second idea was personal and individual and reveals his interest in intellectual culture. He wished his monks to devote themselves, with him, to study, to the copying of manuscripts, to the creation of a library. He seems to have foreseen the loss of the treasures of antiquity if no one attempted to save them, and would himself be their saviour.

# THE CHRISTIAN LATIN LITERATURE OF

Cassiodorus wrote a great deal whilst yet in the world, but only on secular subjects: a *Universal Chronicle*, from the Creation to 519, a vague compilation, containing much from S. Jerome and Prosper; a *History of the Goths*, in twelve books, which we only know from the abridgment of Jordanis; twelve books of *Variæ* (*Epistolæ*) published between 534 and 538; these are official letters written by Cassiodorus in the name of Theodoric and his successors, or in his own name, and are of considerable historical interest; they number more than 400. He also wrote a small treatise, *De Anima*, which does not possess much originality.

It was chiefly during his life at Vivarium that Cassiodorus devoted himself to literary labours. He had translated by one of his friends, Epiphanius the Scholastic, the three Histories of Socrates, Sozomen and Theodoret, and from the three he composed a unique *Historia Tripartita*. He wrote *Enarrationes in Psalmos*, founded on S. Augustine, Commentaries on the Acts of the Apostles and the Apocalypse and presided over a vast laboratory of translations, whence issued Latin versions of Clement of Alexandria, *Adumbrationes in Epistolas canonicas*; of Origen's Homilies on Esdras; of Didymus, *In Epistolas canonicas Enarratio*; of S. John Chrysostom's Homilies on the Epistle to the Hebrews; of the documents relating to the Council of Chalcedon, etc. But his greatest work is undoubtedly the *Institutiones divinarum et sæcularium litterarum*. The first book of this work deals with the study of the Bible: it is good to read the Holy Scriptures, but it is better to understand them, and Cassiodorus explains to his monks

## THE FIRST SIX CENTURIES

how to attain to their understanding. He reminds them that here the knowledge of the secular sciences is indispensable, and that without their assistance one may meet with insuperable difficulties. At the same time he encourages them to make copies of the Sacred Books and gives wise counsels as to the rules for this work. In the second book, which is much shorter, the author speaks of the seven liberal arts, grammar, rhetoric, dialectics, arithmetic, music, geometry and astronomy, and describes their objects and methods, according to the theoricians of antiquity.

The *Institutions* of Cassiodorus may be called the spiritual testament of the ancient culture. They organize, as far as was possible, the transmission of the precious legacy of former literature. Before being completely invaded by the Barbarians the old world finds refuge in the cloister, where, at least, in the monastic libraries shall be preserved what remains of the best of the ancient writings. The *Institutions* cannot be called a masterpiece, but neither should we try to lower their significance and their influence.

### IV. Saint Gregory the Great

After Cassiodorus only one Italian writer remains to be noticed—the great Pope, S. Gregory. He was born in Rome, of an ancient Roman family, about 450. He, too, began with an official career, but, like so many others, after a time felt drawn to a life of perfection. He sold his goods, founded seven monasteries and retired to one of them, on the Cælian Hill. He did not long remain there, for the reigning Popes wished to employ him. One of the seven deacons (*regionarii*) of Rome under Benedict I, and *apocrisianus*, or permanent ambassador at Constantinople under Pelagius II, on the death of the latter Gregory was elected Pope.

Then began that wonderful period of fruitful and incessant activity which made S. Gregory's Pontificate the greatest in the history of the Church. By and through him Faith was upheld against heresy and schism, discipline was restored, the liturgy and sacred chant reorganized, the poor better assisted, the patrimony of the Church administered with justice and prudence; England evangelized, the pretensions of the Patriarch of Constantinople repressed, and the splendour of the Papacy revealed to the world. When this great Pope died, on the 12th March, 604, he left a work the solidity of which would be proved to future generations.

It has been justly said that the chief characteristic of Gregory's genius was a practical good sense, enabling him always to keep the exact mean and showing him on every occasion the best path to follow. This great Roman had inherited the gift of governing men; he knew how to demand of each only what he could give, and never to expect of any person more than he had power to supply. When the Patriarch of Constantinople assumed the title of Æcumenical Bishop, to which he had no right, Gregory replied to him as "the servant of the servants of God," thus manifesting his deep humility and the religious view he took of his mission; certain, through his knowledge of men, of obtaining more by his moderation than would the Patriarch by his arrogance. His written works show the same qualities: precision, moderation,

## THE FIRST SIX CENTURIES

calm, and a rectitude of judgment that belong to none but the great leaders of men.

It is surprising that in such a busy life Gregory should have found time to write. He has nevertheless left a number of works. The most important and interesting are his correspondence. This includes about eight hundred letters, covering the whole of his Pontificate and dealing with all the anxieties and interests of his daily life. Thanks to these letters we learn in detail the many duties and tasks of a Pope who is worthy of the name. Standing alone, in the midst of ruins, the Church strives to preserve all that still remains and to conquer for Christ the new races that are taking possession of Europe. Gregory gives untiring attention to this great work. His letters, long preserved by the Roman Chancery, have been many times copied: a collection, addressed to Charlemagne by Pope Adrian I, has preserved the most important of them.

The *Commentary on Job*, begun when Gregory was *apocrisarius* at Constantinople, but only finished after 590, consists of thirty-five books. It is a considerable work, in which the text of Scripture serves as the foundation for a long series of moral reflections. The book is consequently better known as the *Morals*, from its teaching on Christian ethics.

We have specimens of S. Gregory's preaching in forty homilies on the Gospels and twenty-two on Ezechiel. These sermons are specially remarkable by their simplicity and familiar tone. The orator speaks to his people, not to astonish, but to edify. He draws from his predecessors, notably S. Ambrose and S. Augustine, but his tone is none the less original. Many fragments of the homilies have been introduced into the liturgy, and they have greatly influenced the pastoral eloquence of later centuries.

Two ascetic works have been even more widely read than the sermons: the *Liber Pastoralis Curæ* and the *Dialogues*. The *Pastoral* is addressed chiefly to the clergy and explains the duties of a bishop. It is in some sort the Latin equivalent of S. John Chrysostom's treatise on the priesthood. Its four books study successively the conditions under which the pastoral charge ought to be accepted, the virtues the bishop should practise and the works he should undertake, the teaching he should give by word and example, and, lastly, the constant watch he should keep upon himself by the examination of his conscience. This work has always been proposed to clerics as the best guide for their moral life. Translated into Greek by the Patriarch of Antioch, Anastasius II, into Anglo-Saxon by King Alfred, and recommended by many councils, it held a considerable place in the formation of the medieval clergy.

The *Dialogues* were written for the edification of the people. S. Gregory there relates the miracles worked in Italy at the intercession of the Saints, particularly of S. Benedict, to whom the whole book is dedicated. One hardly knows which most to admire in this work; the simplicity of the narrator, who relates without flinching the most extraordinary stories, or the credulity of those who were intended to read them. The *Dialogues* have no critical pretensions; they are simply anecdotes, related as such, with the most charming bonhomie. Like his contemporaries, Gregory must have believed them; but he never goes below the surface, and it is just this that makes the charm of the book which has delighted many generations of Christians and still continues to edify its readers.

The liturgy and ecclesiastical chant appear to have been carefully revised by S. Gregory, but it is difficult to assign his exact share in what is known as the *Gregorian Sacramentary*. The work that bears this title is taken from a copy sent by Pope Adrian I to Charlemagne, between 784 and 791, and it is probable that this edition had undergone certain modifications since Gregory's time.

We must not seek for great regard to form in S. Gregory's works. The Latin spoken and written by this great Pope is such as we should expect to find at that time when the old world was crumbling to pieces. But it is simple and homely, and the new words and barbarous expressions need not be taken into account. And why, indeed, should S. Gregory seek to compose works of art, seeing that both he and his contemporaries were possessed with the idea that the world was speedily coming to an end? "Behold," he declared, "the world is withering away; death is everywhere, mourning is everywhere, and desolation. The end of temporal things shows how worthless is all that passes; the fall of creatures proves that they were but transitory, even while they seemed to be eternal."

Nevertheless the world still lasts, and we can still read the works of the great Pope who witnessed with such strength and courage the dissolution of the ancient universe.

# CHAPTER XV

### GAUL AND SPAIN

I. Theologians and Controversialists. II. Saint Gregory of Tours. III. The Spaniards. IV. Saint Isidore of Seville.

As in Africa and Italy, so in Gaul decline was rapid from the second half of the fifth century. Faustus of Riez and Salvianus of Marseilles were good writers whose language was correct and easy. S. Gregory of Tours himself confesses that he was unlettered, that he often took masculine for feminine and inversely, that he did not employ prepositions correctly, and that his writings gave the effect of a bull playing at *palæstra*. We must now traverse this last path of decline.

## *I. Theologians and Controversialists*

Faustus of Riez was of British origin, but he studied at Lérins, whence, in 452, he was taken to be made Bishop of Riez. His great virtue and theological knowledge soon caused him to be regarded as an authority by his contemporaries, and these same gifts were the cause of his being driven into exile by the Arian King, Enric, about

# THE CHRISTIAN LATIN LITERATURE

478. However, after the King's death he was able to return to his diocese, where he remained till his death.

Gennadius has left us a sufficiently complete catalogue of Faustus' works, but we do not find there all the writings that have come down to us under his name. The treatises, *On the Holy Ghost*, *On Grace*, and *On the Reason of Faith* are certainly genuine. Some letters and discourses complete his literary inheritance, though there may be other sermons in the apocryphal or anonymous collections. What he has left shows him to have been a devoted bishop, a theologian with semi-Pelagian leanings and inclined to believe in the corporeity of angels and human souls. He was a writer without warmth, but not without elegance.

Of his contemporaries, Leontius of Arles and Rusticius of Limoges, we have only some letters. Claudianus Mamertus, a poet of Vienne, has left a curious treatise: *De Statu Animæ*, directed against Faustus, to prove that human souls are wholly spiritual beings.

Salvianus of Marseilles, probably born near Cologne, at the end of the fifth century, was, like many others, attracted by the reputation of the monks of Lérins and Marseilles. He died in the latter town, about 480, after a long and honoured life. Nevertheless Salvianus was an unsound writer, incapable of preserving a true mean and whose absolute theses sometimes shock the reader. Thus, under the pretext of writing *Against Avarice*, he maintains that all Christians are bound to leave their property to the Church, if they wish to obtain pardon for their sins. Again, in *The Government of God* he contrasts the great virtues of the Barbarians with the vices and sins of the Romans, who, for their depravity, have deserved to lose the empire of the world. Like S. Augustine and Orosius, Salvianus desired to explain the invasions and the fall of Rome, and, like them, would justify the action of Providence, but whilst his predecessors retained in their hearts the love of *Romania*, his admiration is only for the invaders. It is a new position, and the violence with which it is defended fails to hide its weakness. But Salvianus is not destitute of eloquence; and the arguments he employs in favour of his paradox merits the esteem of the lettered.

We have several times mentioned the name of Gennadius of Marseilles, and in fact we owe to him most of our knowledge of the Christian writers of the fifth century. No details are known of his life, and his works are lost, with the exception of a small book: *De ecclesiasticis dogmatibus*, which may perhaps be the conclusion of a more important work on heresies, and, above all of a catalogue: *De Viris illustribus*, which is a continuation of S. Jerome's work. Such catalogues have no literary value, but the information they contain makes them indispensable. In spite of his ignorance and errors Gennadius is our surest guide for the literature of the fifth century.

During the first half of the sixth century S. Cæsarius of Arles is the chief representative of the Gallican episcopate. Born at Chalon-sur-Saône in 470, twenty years later a monk of Lérins, he became Bishop of Arles in 503, and taught and directed the whole of Christian Gaul for forty years. He interested himself in doctrinal questions and obtained the condemnation of semi-Pelagianism by the second Council of Orange, in 529. But he occupied himself

## THE FIRST SIX CENTURIES

more with questions of morals and discipline, and it is as a preacher that he is chiefly famous. In order to help priests in the ministry he made collections of sermons for their use: the homilies of S. Augustine are there placed beside his own, without, however, any acknowledgment of the fact, the essential point being to help ignorant priests to preach usefully. This explains why the greater number of S. Cæsarius' sermons have come down to us anonymously, or under S. Augustine's name and that of others. This renders the task of criticism complicated, and the fine work of Dom Morin has not yet concluded the clearance of the ground. As far as we know him, S. Cæsarius is an admirable type of the popular preacher: he speaks to his people briefly, in familiar language; he explains the great truths of Christian life with a smiling ease that does not exclude austerity, and his homilies are a valuable witness to the life of Christianity in Southern Gaul in the sixth century.

Besides the sermons Cæsarius has left some letters and some short writings on Grace, as well as two monastic rules, one for men and one for virgins. The drawing-up of rules for convents was at that time occupying many. Not long after Cæsarius, Aurelian of Arles and Ferreolus of Uzes wrote some similar rules, and a treatise of Julian Pomerius *On the Contemplative Life*, is also intended for souls desirous of perfection.

### II. Saint Gregory of Tours

S. Cœsarius of Arles was finishing his laborious career when Gregory was born at Clermont, in

## THE CHRISTIAN LATIN LITERATURE OF

Auvergne, on the 30th November, 538. His education, under the direction of a bishop and a priest, was wholly clerical, and he was more familiar with the Bible and the Christian writers than with secular authors. He felt the effects of this education throughout his life; he could not but be an uncultured writer, puzzled by the most elementary rules of syntax, unable to give their correct meaning to words; but as he had a remarkably gifted mind, these defects of form were redeemed by the brilliant qualities of a narrator which turn his works into vivid pictures.

He became Bishop of Tours in 573. The office was a particularly difficult one, as at that time Tours was the religious centre of Gaul and all eyes turned instinctively to the ruler of that illustrious Church. Gregory did not become S. Martin's successor without hesitation, but once accepted, he showed himself worthy of his mission. For the space of twenty years he was a bishop wholly devoted to the interests of his diocese and of the Catholic Church. Whether he had to resist the pretensions of King Chilperic, to practise charity towards the poor, to re-establish discipline where it had decayed, or to convert the heathen, Gregory was ready for every duty. When he died, on the 7th November, 593 or 594, it was with the reputation of a Saint, and the Church has endorsed that reputation.

In spite of his many apostolic labours, Gregory found time to write *A Book on the Psalter*, of which only fragments remain; another, *De Cursu Stellarum ratio*, written to fix, according to the position of the principal constellations, the time for saying the Offices of the Church. He also wrote two books on the miracles of S. Andrew and S. Thomas, a

## THE FIRST SIX CENTURIES

translation of the Passion of the Seven Sleepers at Ephesus, and above all, seven books of *Miracles* and the *History of the Franks*.

The seven books of *Miracles* are a collection rather than a single work. First comes the *Book of the Glories of the Martyrs*, containing the miracles of Our Lord, the Apostles and the martyrs of Gaul; then follow a book on the miracles of S. Julian of Brioude, and four on the miracles of S. Martin of Tours: the book on *The Lives of the Fathers*, which relates in twenty chapters the histories of twenty-three Saints of Gaul, was first published separately and afterwards added to the first collection. Lastly a book, *In gloria Confessorum*, forms a supplement to the first " *Glories* " and completes the collection.

All these accounts are full of information on popular devotion and piety in the sixth century. Gregory relates what he has seen and heard spoken of, without criticism; he calmly reports the most extraordinary occurrences, and for the most part evidently shares the simple faith of his readers, though occasionally a half-smile seems to show that he is not quite so credulous as he appears. The Saints of Gaul, whose tombs he had visited, interest him particularly: they are not now very well known and the pious bishop's revival of their glory is all the more charming.

S. Gregory's fame as an historian rests on his *Historia Francorum*. He begins his account at the Creation, and for all the first part contents himself with a chronological summary down to the death of S. Martin. The later books grow more and more detailed as they relate to contemporary events of which the writer had personal knowledge. With the fifth book Gregory enters into minute personal details, and the *History* takes the form and proportions of *Memoirs*. The good Bishop depicts persons he has known, acknowledges his sympathies and antipathies, and gives prominence to events according as they affect his Church or himself. He does not attempt to reason or comprehend, but relates leisurely, dwelling longer on what is most beautiful. His *History* is an indispensable guide to those scholars who have no other contemporary work at hand, and is especially a work of predilection for those who love beautiful stories.

### III. The Spaniards

It was long before Spain embraced Christianity; isolated by her geographical situation, at the extreme end of the Christian republic, she never held an important place in the history of the Church or of Christian literature, in spite of Ossius of Cordova or Prudentius. The Barbarian invasions increased her isolation, all the more that they were so severely felt. The invaders could go no further, and Spain became the battle-field of the Alani, the Suevi, Vandals, Goths and Heruli, and it was long before even a relative peace could be established in this unhappy country. Such conditions could scarcely be favourable for the development of literature, and it is not surprising that few names are worth recording.

Amongst the most interesting are the chroniclers. Hydatius, Bishop of Aquæ Flaviæ in Galicia is the author of a *Chronicle* in continuation of S. Jerome's, from 379 to 468; dating from 427, it is one of the most valuable sources for the history of the Church

## THE FIRST SIX CENTURIES

in Spain. A century later John of Biclaro wrote a continuation of the Chronicle of Victor of Tunnuna for the period between 567-590; these annals are also full of information.

Exegesis is only represented by Apringius of Bija, who wrote a Commentary, now lost, on the Apocalypse, and by Justus of Urgel, the author of an allegorical explanation of the Canticle of Canticles. In theology we find the names of Turribius of Astorga, who took part in the Priscillian controversies, of Severus of Malaga, who combated Arianism, of Justinian of Valencia, who wrote a *Book in reply to Rusticius*, of Licinian of Cartagena, who taught the corporeity of the angels, and of Eutropius of Valencia, a zealous narrator of monastic life. All this, as we see, is not very much.

Better known and more worth knowing is Martin of Braga, one of the most striking personages of that troubled period. He was born in Pannonia and lived in Palestine, where he became a monk; finally he went to Galicia and was first Abbot of a monastery and then Bishop of Dumio. In 572 he became Archbishop of Braga and played a very important part in the conversion of the Suevi. Martin was extraordinarily learned for his time: amongst profane writers Seneca was his favourite; he strove to imitate him and was not unsuccessful. His books, *Formula Vitæ honestæ, De Ira, Pro repellanda Jactantia, De Superbia, Exhortatio Humilitatis*, clearly reveal his long acquaintance with the pagan moralist, though he makes the most laudable efforts to Christianize his doctrine.

The book *On the Conversion of the Peasants* is more interesting and personal, and is full of curious information on the religious and moral condition of the country people. It is a sort of manual for the pastoral visitation of bishops; Martin wrote it at the request of one of them, Polemius of Astorga, and in it the Archbishop indicates what seem to him the best means of combating idolatry. He thereby reveals the influence still exercised by paganism on the peasants of Spain so many centuries after the birth of Christianity. We also possess a letter of the Archbishop on *Triple Immersion*, a writing *On Easter*, a collection of conciliar canons and a translation of the apophthegms of the Fathers. All this work denotes a more than common intellectual activity.

### IV. Saint Isidore of Seville

The fame of Martin is quite eclipsed by that of S. Isidore of Seville, who, with Boethius, Cassiodorus and S. Gregory the Great, was one of the initiators of the Middle Ages. He was the son of Severianus and the brother of Leander, his predecessor in the See of Seville. Leander was also very learned, as we find from a Homily on the triumph of the Church and a small work addressed to his sister Florentina, on the consecration of virgins and contempt of the world. But Isidore was a far greater scholar. He read, remembered and noted everything, and was a living encyclopedia; in his person was concentrated all the knowledge of antiquity. In order to share this knowledge with his contemporaries he compiled, in twenty books, an immense work, to which he gave the title of

## THE FIRST SIX CENTURIES

*Etymologiæ*, or *Origines*. The mere enumeration of the titles of these books is bewildering: grammar, rhetoric, dialectic; the four mathematical subjects (arithmetic, geometry, music and astronomy); medicine; law and chronology (including a universal chronicle down to 627); ecclesiastical books and offices; God, the angels and men; the Church and various sects; languages, peoples, kingdoms; etymology (*vocum certarum alphabetum*); man and monsters; animals; the world and its parts; houses and fields; stones and metals; agriculture; war and games; ships, houses and clothes; food, instruments and tools. It would probably be useless to seek the reason or method of this distribution of subjects. Rather let us admire the serenity with which Isidore undertook the task of treating so many different subjects, and marvel still more at his success. For there is no doubt that the *Etymologies* are a success. We must not of course judge them according to our modern ideas. The place held by the science of etymology—and such a science!—is surprising, as are many other things in the collection. But there is so much learning and experience, and, we may add, such good faith, that we can only bow before it. The Middle Ages did no less. The *Etymologies* were for centuries the chief manual or text-book in educational institutions. Many times copied, studied and summarized, it would be difficult to define exactly all that the Western races owe to it.

This vast work, which occupied Isidore for many years and which he had not time to finish, was not the only production of his encyclopedic mind. Two books: *Libri duo Differentiarum*; two *Synonyma*; a treatise *De natura Rerum*; and one *De Ordine*

## THE CHRISTIAN LATIN LITERATURE OF

*Creaturarum* testify to the great scope of his reading and his insatiable desire for knowledge.

A *Chronicon* down to the year 615; the *Historia de Regibus Gothorum, Wandalorum et Suevorum* and *De Viris illustribus*, which, in thirty-three chapters continues the work of Gennadius, are Isidore's contribution to history. He wrote several explanations of Holy Scripture: *De ortu et obitu Patrum qui in Scriptura laudibus efferenda; Allegoriæ quædam Sacræ Scripturæ; Liber numerorum qui in Sanctis Scripturis occurrunt; In libros Veteris et Novo Testamenti Proœmia; De Veteri et Novo Testamento Quæstiones; Secretorum Expositiones Sacramentorum seu questiones in Vetus Testamentum. De Fide Catholica ex Vetu et Novo Testamento contra Judæos* belongs properly speaking to theology, as does a book of *Sentences*, taken from S. Augustine and S. Gregory. To the liturgy belongs the *De ecclesiasticis Officiis*, one of S. Isidore's most interesting works, containing much information on the ancient liturgy of the Church of Spain. Lastly, his ascetic teaching is represented by a *Regula Monachorum* in twenty-four chapters.

It is scarcely necessary to remark that in such an immense output the work is unequal in value. S. Isidore copied much from his predecessors, and without much discernment. He took his matter as he found it, and scarcely troubled to make sure of its worth. But it is well that the ancient world did not come to an end till some writer had felt himself capable of recapitulating its lessons, and that writer was S. Isidore. The clarity, one might almost say the simple elegance of his style is not without charm. Many foreign words and expressions are

## THE FIRST SIX CENTURIES

mixed with his Latin, but as a whole the language is more correct than might have been expected.

S. Isidore died in 636 after a very laborious life. Less than twenty years after his death, in 653, the Council of Toledo rendered solemn homage to his memory, recording its admiration in glowing terms:
"The extraordinary doctor, the latest ornament of the Catholic Church, the most learned man of these last ages, always to be named with reverence, Isidore."

Well, the world has lasted longer than the Fathers of Toledo expected, and it has gained a more correct view of S. Isidore of Seville: but his position is nevertheless an admirable one, for he introduces us to the Middle Ages.

CONCLUSION

WITH Boethius, Cassiodorus and S. Gregory the Great, in Italy, Venantius, Fortunatus and S. Gregory of Tours, in France, S. Isidore of Seville in Spain, a great epoch of intellectual life comes to an end. It is now long since the Roman Empire, exhausted through its own weakness as much as by the Barbarian invasions, ended its long agony: but its spirit, language and civilization survived for two centuries. By the year 600 these, also, were dead, and the witnesses of those tragic years believed that they foreshadowed the speedy advent of the Last Judgment and the consummation of all things. They clearly did not foresee that a new world would arise out of the chaos, but that chaos terrified them, beholding how in it the treasures they most valued were disappearing.

The work of which they were the last survivors had been a great and beautiful one. One has only to measure the distance traversed by Christian Latin literature since the first days, or towards the middle of the second century, when unknown and humble believers timidly essayed to translate the Holy Scriptures into the vernacular. The Church then still spoke Greek and looked towards the East as to her cradle, and even her leaders, the Bishops of Rome, were faithful to Hellenism. It was not till

# THE CHRISTIAN LATIN LITERATURE OF

the end of the same century that the West began to recognize itself and gave birth to its first writers. These, happily, were men of letters, formed in the best schools of Roman Africa, profoundly imbued with classical culture, and endowed, though not all in the same degree, with real talent. Whilst, until the fourth century the Greek Church had merely occasional writers, who were ignorant of style, even while they despised it, the Latin Church possessed in Tertullian, his contemporaries and immediate successors, men who had learnt to speak and write and who understood the strength that could be given to an argument by a well-constructed sentence or happy phrase. Some of these writers were veritable rhetoricians, but they surpassed their rivals of the pagan schools by the inspirations of Faith, that saved them from being content with empty sounds. Some, like Tertullian and S. Cyprian, stand as masters. The *Apologeticus* of Tertullian, and the *Letters* of S. Cyprian may be safely compared to the finest works of profane literature; they rank far above all contemporary writings and belong to those of the best authors.

When the Edict of Milan brought peace to the Church Christian Latin literature already possessed her own traditions and might be content to follow her models of the third century. Some of her best representatives towards the end of the fourth century had begun to study the question of the use of profane authors: S. Jerome, after his famous dream, decided definitely against it. Others, like S. Augustine, in his *De Doctrina Christiana*, were less severe, and S. Jerome himself practically continued to read Cicero. All had gone through their studies in the best schools; S. Jerome under

## THE FIRST SIX CENTURIES

Donatus, and Paulinus of Nola under Ausonius. The teaching of such masters is not easy to forget, and when they themselves began to write, classical recollections came, as it were, spontaneously to their minds; this enabled them also to handle the language with skill and to express themselves in a chaste and elegant style.

The legend of the barbarous Latin of the Fathers of the Church has been exploded. Much patient study of the language[1] and the style of S. Ambrose, S. Jerome, S. Augustine and many others has proved that all these writers remained faithful to classic traditions, and that, taking the circumstances into account, they must be regarded as the heirs and successors of the great prose-writers and poets of republican and imperial Rome.

During the Barbarian period this conclusion is even more evident. In the midst of the general ruin the Church alone stands. She, so to speak, crystallizes within herself the aspirations, the memories, the pride and the glory of Rome.

The ancient aristocracy, so long rebellious against Christianity, and which at the end of the fourth century demanded by the mouth of Symmachus the restoration of the altar of Victory in the Hall of the Senate, had now been converted and had found within the Church the best of all that had made Rome great. Whether in the service of the barbarian kings, always ready to profit by their experience, or by devotion to the Church under the ever-increasing burden of the episcopate, these representatives of the old race pursued the same ideals as their ancestors, only purified and ennobled by the virtues of Christianity. The writers whom

[1] *Vocalaire.*

we have been describing belonged to the most illustrious of those ancient families who long preserve their traditions, and these traditions are not only those of government, but also of civilization, literary education, carefulness of language and style. By the force of things these last Roman writers are subjected to barbarian influences; their Latin resembles less and less the Latin of Cicero; they know this and suffer accordingly. The best amongst them strive their utmost against the decline, but their efforts are too manifest, and we behold rhetoric taking the place of true feeling. Others, sighing, accept their helplessness and, like S. Gregory of Tours, resign themselves to employ the language of their contemporaries. They are wise; for by consenting to free themselves from the past they prepare for the future.

At the time of its consummation Patristic Latin literature possessed a vast inheritance of great works. Less speculative and theological than the Greek, it is also far more human. The questions it has posed and answered are not those difficult and mysterious ones on the Trinity or the Incarnation, but those of Divine Grace in its relation to human acts. From Tertullian to Boethius, from S. Cyprian to S. Gregory the Great, this literature deals with the rules of Christian life. Tertullian is a rigorist, who dislikes moderate decisions and boldly declares his "all or nothing" theories. S. Cyprian, to whose episcopal character belongs a juster understanding of the needs of souls, receives the lapsed to penance; S. Ambrose endeavours to adapt the duties of the Stoic ethics—which are also those of all honest men—to the fresh needs of Christianity; S. Augustine, deeply pene-

## THE FIRST SIX CENTURIES

trated with the sense of the necessity of Divine assistance and the gravity of sin, is the Doctor of Grace: he expounds, with unequalled force, the place held by God in the life of each one of us. Boethius seeks consolation in philosophy, and S. Gregory the Great preaches to his flock wisdom, moderation and calm in presence of the upheavals that foretold the end of the ancient world. Each one of these great men, according to his personal temperament and natural affinities, develops the teaching of Christ and strives to lead souls to perfection.

From so many efforts there has resulted the constitution of a rule of morals which is that of the whole Latin Church. The exaggerations of Tertullian have been rejected, and, to a certain extent, some of the severest theses of S. Augustine. Christianity has never denied human liberty or obliged her children to live outside the borders of civil society. Inversely, she has condemned Helvidius and Jovinian, who sought to abase virginity, and, still more, the error of Pelagius, who rejected the assistance of Divine Grace as vain and useless. The Church has always believed in the higher merit of renunciation and in the absolute necessity of Grace. She is moderate in her wisdom and she has her human side, which, however, does not prevent her from pursuing as her ideal the conquest of the Kingdom of Heaven.

We have not inherited only a rule of morals from the Christian Latin writers, but also our manner of thinking, speaking and writing. The literary influence of the Fathers was considerable in the Western world; the early Middle Ages almost lived on the last of them. Boethius, Cassiodorus, S. Gregory

## THE CHRISTIAN LATIN LITERATURE

and Isidore of Seville were for many centuries almost the only teachers of the nations that were being formed on the ruins of the Roman Empire. Whilst Cicero and Virgil were less read, the *Etymologies*, the *Consolations*, the *Dialogues* and the *Institutions* were both read and copied. These books were imitated, compiled, summarized; they even provided subjects for religious art, and one would hardly believe how much the sculptors of the twelfth and thirteenth centuries owed to S. Isidore and S. Gregory.

The Renaissance, which reintroduced the cult of the pagan authors—who had already been honoured and cultivated during the great centuries of the Middle Ages—made her sons unjust to the Christian writers. All they owed to them was forgotten: the many words they had created, the many happy expressions and formulas they had introduced; the modes of thinking and speaking of which they were the authors. These sons of the Renaissance were unwilling to acknowledge that our modern tongues and our whole genius were formed by those early writers.

To-day we seem to be more just in the appreciation of our literary ancestors and we adjudge to them a more correct place in the history of Christian thought and Western civilization.

May this little volume, in which we have endeavoured to write of these early Christian authors with gratitude, help our readers to know and love them better.

# BIBLIOGRAPHY

### EDITIONS AND TEXTS

THE greater number of the works that constitute Christian Latin literature are contained in the *Patrologiæ Latinæ Cursus Completus* of J. P. Migne, in 219 volumes (Paris, 1844-1855). This is not a critical work, but is intended only as a reproduction of the best ancient editions.

The *Corpus Scriptorum Ecclesiasticorum Latinorum*, on the contrary, contains critical editions; it has been published since 1866 by the Academy of Vienne and at present counts 58 volumes. These editions are generally good, but some are insufficient, and should be treated with reserve.

A number of texts, relating to the last period of our History, have appeared in the *Monumenta Germaniæ Historica anotores Antiquissimi*, in 13 volumes (Berlin, 1877-1898). These are also critical editions, and valuable as containing the works of secondary authors neglected by older editors.

### LITERARY HISTORIES

LE NAIN DE TILLEMONT. *Mémoires pour servir a l'histoire ecclésiastique des six premiers siècles;* Paris, 1693-1712.
LES BÉNÉDICTINS DE S. MAUR. *Histoire littéraire de la France,* II-III; Paris, 1733-1735.
BARDENHEWER. *Patrologie,* tr. by Shahan; Freiburg, im Br. S. Louis, 1908
— *Geschicte der altkirchlichen Literatur;* Freiburg, 1902. The 4 volumes that have appeared of this monumental History cover the first five centuries.

# THE CHRISTIAN LATIN LITERATURE

MONCEAUX. *Histoire littéraire de l'Afrique Chrétienne;* Paris, 1901. So far 7 volumes of this great work have been published, from Tertullian to S. Augustine.
TIXERONT. *Précis de Patrologie;* Paris, 1918. There is an English translation of this.
ALLIES. " The Flowering of Patristic Literature," in *The Throne of the Fisherman;* Burns, 1909.
NEWMAN. *Tracts Theological and Ecclesiastical.*
— *Historical Sketches;* London, Longmans.
DE BROGLIE. *S. Ambrose,* tr. by Maitland;
HATZFELD. *S. Augustine,* tr. by Holt. Both these are in " The Saints " Series; Duckworth, 1899.
WISEMAN. *S. Augustine and the Donatists;* in the *Dublin Review; July,* 1839. [This Article became famous, as destroying Newman's theory of the *Via Media* and helping towards his conversion.]

Those English-speaking students of Christian Latin (or Greek) literature who may wish for more information than is contained in this volume, but who may have neither time nor opportunity for consulting long histories or foreign books, will find in the *Catholic Encyclopedia* able and exhaustive Articles on almost all the writers dealt with in this text-book. The value of each Article is enhanced by a Bibliography at the end of each.

www.ingramcontent.com/pod-product-compliance
Lightning Source LLC
LaVergne TN
LVHW041614070426
835507LV00008B/229